THE PERSONA PRINCIPLE ™

How to Succeed in Business With Image-Marketing

Derek Lee Armstrong and Kam Wai Yu

Original illustrations by Raffi Anderian

"A man, in order to establish himself in the world, does everything he can to appear established there."
La Rochefoucauld

Proceeds from the sale of this book provided support for human services to those in need in the Shenandoah Valley of Virginia.

A Fireside Book
Published by Simon & Schuster

Original illustrations by Raffi Anderian.
Photography by Luis Palu, Mark Stegel and Rob Allen.

We gratefully acknowledge all of our valued clients and especially wish to recognize the companies illustrated in this book (listed in order of appearance): IBM Canada Limited, The Academy of Canadian Cinema and Television, Letraset Canada—a Division of Esselte Canada Inc., CCNS Corporate Services Limited, The Ontario Ministry of Economic Development, Trade and Tourism, Fairview Mall, Lonix Hats and Parktown Hat and Cap Ltd. IBM packaging courtesy of IBM Canada Limited. IBM and AS/400® are registered trademarks of IBM Canada Limited. The Information Place™ is a trademark of CCNS Corporate Services Limited. Lonix™ and Adventure Hats™ are trademarks of Parktown Hat and Cap Ltd. All other trademarks mentioned or shown in this book are the property of their respective owners.

FIRESIDE
Rockefeller Center
1230 Avenue of the Americas
New York, NY 10020

First Fireside Edition 1997
FIRESIDE and colophon are registered trademarks of Simon & Schuster Inc.
Designed by Two Dimensions; Advertising by Design
Manufactured in the United States of America
10   9   8   7   6   5   4   3   2   1

The Library of Congress has cataloged the Simon & Schuster edition as follows:
Armstrong, Derek Lee.
The persona principle : how to succeed in business with image-marketing / Derek Lee Armstrong and Kam Wai Yu.—1st ed.
p.   cm.
1. Success in business. 2. Corporate image. 3. Advertising. 4. Marketing—Management. 5. Sales promotion. I. Yu, Kam Wai. II. Title.
HF5386.A736   1996
650.1—dc20   95-42915 CIP

ISBN 0-684-80268-6
ISBN 0-684-80269-4 (pbk)

CONTENTS

CONTENTS

CONTENTS

CONTENTS

CONTENTS

IS PERSONA
FOR YOU?

▼

*"A man must ride alternately on
the horses of his private and his public nature."*
Ralph Waldo Emerson

The Conduct of Life

Why You Need A Persona Plan

Less than 26 percent of business marketers develop an annual marketing communications plan.[1] Even though these business people know they should prepare an annual plan, 58 percent failed to do it because of lack of expertise and 48 percent because of lack of budget.

The Persona Principle was designed to overcome these specific weaknesses inherent in 74 percent of all ventures: lack of marketing expertise and lack of budget.

These Secrets Are Worth Billions

Companies have earned billions of dollars using the Image-Marketing secrets of The Persona Principle. Carefully crafted Persona Plans have built companies and revitalized failing brands. The Persona Principle has *never* failed when executed correctly.

The Persona Principle does not require big bank accounts. It does not even require that you be "the best." Persona requires only that you follow your own Persona Plan faithfully. Your success is almost certainly assured—provided your claims are true—if you follow all the steps of the Persona Planning Process.

Persona Is For Everyone

The mathematical models of our tested Persona Planning Process are built around the needs of all sizes and types of business ventures— from start-up to large corporation. The Persona Principle was engineered to a standard format that is indexed for any size venture. You don't need marketing knowledge to benefit from the program. And you don't need a large budget.

The principles contained in this book can be easily applied to success in many areas:

★ Entrepreneurial start-ups.
★ Salesperson development.
★ Branding of products.
★ Employee advancement in the workplace.
★ Personal development of image to achieve goals.

The eight most important chapters of this book are the Persona Factors, which contain tips for: business people, entrepreneurs, salespeople, employees, and individuals (for use in their personal lives).

The Road to Success

The route is not easy, but it is mapped. There are at least eighty-eight potential roadblocks to your success. These eighty-eight roadblocks are described in this book, one by one, as the 88 Persona Codes. Each Persona Code describes how to avoid the obstacles to your success. With these trademarked concepts, you will succeed in your objectives—if your objectives are realistic and you follow all the steps of the Persona Principle.

The Biggest Obstacle to Your Success

The biggest obstacle to your success is invisibility. The best, the most experienced, or the most talented cannot enjoy prosperity until they are visible to their potential market.

This is a profound truth for any venture, person, or business. Becoming visible at a party can lead to romance. Becoming visible in the workplace can bring a long overdue promotion. Becoming visible to your prospects can bring corporate success.

There are several ways to become visible:
* ★ Spend excessive amounts of money to reach your prospective customers (advertising).
* ★ Scream and shout your truth until someone listens (public relations).
* ★ Get a lucky break (don't hold your breath).
* ★ Build equity in your image through the science of the Persona Principle.

The Secret of Visibility

Becoming visible is only the first highway to travel on your route to true success. The route you choose can determine the duration of your triumph.

A lucky break can bring success—but it is usually very short-lived. A massive spending spree in advertising or promotions will certainly pull customers—until you stop spending. You can use negative or positive public relations, demanding people notice you—but the persona created for your venture will be out of your control.

The secret to stable and long-term success is Image-Marketing. There are eighty-eight Image-Marketing concepts and eight important Persona Factors contained in the trademarked science of the Persona Principle. This is the only specific step-by-step process that contains all the known factors and variables in image-building. It is the scientific and certain way to build the equity value of your image.

The concept is a simple one: your very first priority should be to invest in your image. Don't spend or shout your way to the top. Spending is only a way of reaching your audience. There are inexpensive and expensive ways of achieving notoriety. Steadily investing in your image is the inexpensive way. In time, your image will become an icon. Using all of the techniques, tips, instructions, and formulas of the Persona Principle can make you the Xerox of your industry.

The Second Obstacle

The second roadblock on your journey to success is credibility. This is a major factor, which is extensively covered in the Persona Planning Process. Building a strong image on no substance will bring only short-term success. Just as investing in risky stocks is usually wasteful, investing in an image-only venture is doomed to fail.

Build your image only on credible truths. It is important that you identify and promote only your strengths and your truths. If you can't be the best overall, Persona can help you find your unique niche—a niche in which you can be the best. Everyone, and every venture, can be best at something. Once you've discovered your strengths—through a research process we call your Persona Inventory—you can build an image that will last.

Persona Profile: The Most Famous Brands Are Image Brands

Kleenex. Xerox. Escalator. Alka-Seltzer. Coke. These brands have become synonymous with their functions. We don't grab a tissue, we grab a Kleenex. We don't get a soda, we get a Coke. This is Imaging at its finest. Coca-Cola can open a franchise anywhere in the world and succeed on name alone.

In the forties we saw the rise of some of the greatest personas of all time:

★ Gillette become famous with its "Look sharp, feel sharp" radio jingle.

★ Texaco became a household word with spots on the Milton Berle Show and its Metropolitan Opera sponsorship.

The fifties were also a prolific Persona age:

★ Little Speedy, the animated tablet, built Alka-Seltzer's image into one of the biggest moneymaking names with a "plop, plop, fizz, fizz."

★ Timex did its best with its famous series of ads showing that its watches "keep on ticking."

In the sixties:

★ Maxwell House began percolating on TV with its brilliant "Good to the last drop" campaign, which continued for decades.

★ Hertz became synonymous with rental cars when its leading edge special effects "put you in the driver's seat."

In the seventies:

★ Volkswagen made its mark with a well-remembered TV spot showing a funeral procession for a tycoon who left his money to a thrifty nephew driving a Beetle.

★ Xerox became a household word even outside the office, with Brother Dominic producing 500 copies of his hand-lettered religious manuscript.

These names burn in history because they have equity. A photocopy is a Xerox. Overnight delivery is FedEx. These brands own their categories so completely that competitors can never truly rival them. Pepsi may be a giant in its own right, but it will always be second to Coca-Cola (in fact, in the eighties Pepsi chose to reinforce its number two positioning by building its brand on "taste test" comparisons with Coke! See Persona Code 84, the Code of Twos).

These brands did not become great simply through spending or advertising. While advertising is a great image tool, advertising the wrong message will not build a successful venture, no matter how much you spend. The great brand names are the ones that invested in their carefully crafted images.

Why the Underdog Wins

The underdog is usually the innovator. In war, the oppressed and outnumbered always develop new weapons and strategies to survive. Marketing is not just analogous to warfare—it *is* warfare.

We developed the Persona Principle from our work with many underdog companies, including our own. What began as informal observation became an obsession. We realized that all ventures—of any size or style—benefit equally from the basic principles of Image-Marketing:

★ Our own company, Two Dimensions: Advertising by Design, grew an average of 300 percent per year for five years using the Persona Principle. Using only the Persona Codes—and no start-up capital—Two Dimensions became rated number one in Canada for creativity and is now in the top 6 percent of advertising agencies in Canada by revenue.

★ Using these exclusive Persona Codes, we have launched major new products for all sizes of companies—generating an average of 65 percent above projected target results.

★ The Persona Principle has successfully launched several under funded start-up companies—all of which are prospering.

★ The Persona Principle has resuscitated failing brands and corporations.

A Two-Dimensional Model

Two Dimensions: Advertising by Design was founded on enthusiasm and experience—but no money. Zero. Yet from the beginning, we aggressively staked our true claim that we were the best creative marketing experts available. We knew this to be absolutely true. Our years of working as marketers and creative directors for other firms had taught us important lessons. We knew we were better than anyone else in our field. So we applied easy lesson number one (see Persona Code 21, Code of Horn Blowing):

Never stop telling your audience how good you are.

We became the number one strategic-creative agency in Canada within five years, using this and the other eighty-seven Persona Codes. We have used our carefully built Image-Equity to soar into the top 6 percent of all ad agencies by revenue. We did all of this with no capital investment, no money, and no assets beyond our talent. What money we spent reaching our audience was taken from our revenue. We grew a balance of zero into millions in five years.

Two Dimensions became the final model for Persona. The lessons learned before we formed our company were eagerly and religiously applied to our company:

★ We never showed our weaknesses (which were many in the first two years).
★ We never allowed prospective clients to visit our "virtual" office.
★ We never did anything unless it could be done perfectly (which meant we turned down many jobs, even in the first year, when we needed revenue).
★ We established our persona from the first day, never compromising our fees, our advice, or our principles for any client or prospect. This takes guts, since you have to be willing to walk away from big-dollar business to stand up for your principles.

A Foundation of Truth

All of our claims were true. We knew we were the very best creative marketing people in Canada. If we couldn't claim to be the best creative marketers, then we would have found something else we could have been the best at. The important first step is finding something at which you can honestly claim to be the best. We had a truth foundation to build on. But no dough. Not even a decent car. This is usually a recipe for "give up and get a job." Not Two Dimensions. We were the best. We just had to let everyone know—to become visible.

The first job was for ourselves. We created the best possible logo for our company—an image that represented what we hoped to be in two or three years. It had to be forward-thinking. Logos last at least twenty years, on average, and must have long-term value. We spent weeks drawing and redrawing logos until we were happy. We doodled logos on restaurant napkins. We drew logos on newspapers. We didn't even have a computer to play with; just a pencil and whatever scrap of paper was handy.

Our logo also personified our image of success. It was a spectacular persona statement. Our famous 2D splash defined the funky-fun character of a leading-edge firm.

Our logo also gave us instant credibility. We printed inexpensive business cards, and suddenly we were in business. All we had was a logo and our eagerness to become a number one player in advertising. Most advertising firms are started with millions of dollars in investment start-up capital. We had a logo. Derek dry cleaned his only suit and set out to pitch our services. He told anyone who would listen that Two Dimensions were the best. He told them so many times that eventually prospects began to believe it. He even played a little hard to get to intrigue prospects, turning down dozens of small jobs that were offered to test our abilities. Persona demands that you set your standard from the beginning and never vary from it. We were determined that we would be a top contender. A leading-edge firm would never take small test jobs. One of his first lines in an early 1988 meeting was "We're the most expensive in Canada, but we're worth it." This scared away many prospects, but it succeeded in attracting the type of customer we wanted. This method is what we call Persona-Positioning. Even in the weeks when we despaired over getting a job to pay the bills, we stuck to our standards.

After weeks of cold calling prospects, Derek got an appointment. He drove his beat-up car to the client's office, parked the heap two blocks away so no one would see it, and arrived early enough to comb his hair in the public washroom. Then he played hard to get in the meeting. The prospect believed that if we were willing to walk, we must be good. And Derek was willing to walk. Hungry or not, you have to stand behind your statements.

Success Breeds Success

Our first few jobs could have paid for a new office and a trip to Europe. Instead, our early revenue went straight into our first brochure—a splashy, spotty, expensive brochure. We completely drained our bank account. The production-only cost was an extravagant $48,000 to create only 3,000 brochures! This is an extraordinary sum for a pair of struggling marketers who worked out of a house. Persona came first. Food came last. Our Persona Plan demanded a show-off piece to showcase our talent. We didn't have a dramatic portfolio yet, because we were a start-up. But we had to show our prospects how good we were.

"Spots," as we named the brochure, would represent a dangerous gamble to some. Spending all the company's reserve on one persona piece seemed very risky. We even added extra value to our show-off piece by convincing printers and film houses to sponsor our brochure, promising it would win dozens of international awards. With this promise of publicity, they donated an additional $30,000 in in-kind services.

Our bold Persona tactic brought us $300,000 in revenue within four months. Based on a persona of a "leading-edge, Number One Creative Agency," our brochure won many international awards, as well as the hearts and attention of clients and media. It's even become a permanent reference in big libraries. It is a testament to image-building science at its best. We never doubted that our strategy would work. Two Dimensions was so successful that the

Photography from "Spots" brochure supported the fun and funky Persona of Two Dimensions.

This historical Victorian house was part of Two Dimensions' "creative" persona.

Victorian brownstone in which our company was housed became our trademark. We were fun, funky, creative, strategic. No one wore a suit. Even though the house became crowded as we quickly grew —with average desk space of six square feet—we resisted moving. Our Victorian house with its lovingly tended gardens was our statement about who we were. Eventually, we were forced to move to a much larger building, but a painting of our original Victorian brownstone hangs in the entrance, reminding us of our persona roots.

The Persona Principle became the focus of all of our marketing efforts. After the first five years our company's growth slowed down from a five-year annual average of 300 percent revenue growth to a more sustainable 87 percent. The birth of Two Dimensions, in which we turned our true claim into a marketable persona and then into a runaway success, was aided solely by our application of techniques from the Persona Principle.

Now, instead of beat-up cars, both partners drive luxury automobiles. Our office has moved twice, each time quadrupling in size. Our staff has grown to many times the original size, and we share our substantial profits with each member. We are comfortably wealthy. We take at least four international vacations per year, and we own several houses, buildings, and expensive pieces of real estate. We have applied the Persona Principle to create two other successful corporations. Our own corporations were grown without debt. We use debt only for cash-flow operations and real estate— never for growth. We invested only in our persona image for growth. Our liabilities are a fraction of our assets. And none of our assets is as important as our Persona Image-Equity.

Persona marketing skills represent a science anyone can apply. All the lessons we have learned and key steps to success we have taken are contained in this book.[2]

A Controversial Foundation

The Persona Principle may seem controversial, since the system is based on these truths:
* Image is power.
* Be perceived as the best and you will become the best.
* Your reputation is more important than your bank account.
* There is more value in appearing successful than in being successful.

These are all controversial statements in the 1990s. Marketers are doing all they can to avoid the appearance of hype. The Persona Principle states that image is more valuable than resources or skills to any aspiring entrepreneur, salesperson, manager, or corporate officer. This will be a relief to the underfunded, no-capital, start-up entrepreneur, but it is a notion that will be hotly contested by pundits who believe that we are moving away from the excessive hype of the late twentieth century.

A New Millennium

We are approaching a new millennium—an age many claim will be an era of substance over hype. Marketing gurus forecast a society that will resist hype and demand responsibility and truth.

The image-over-substance controversy is a zero issue. While Persona places more value on image, truth is almost as important. The Persona Principle maintains that if your truth is never visible to your potential clients, you will fail. For every success story, there are dozens of failures. Most failures are not due to lack of talent, substance, or value. We have studied many failing companies and, without exception, they were quality offerings. They failed because they were invisible.

All ventures must present a targeted and focused persona to their prospective customers. No venture, no matter how heroic, can afford to be anonymous. Remember, it is far better to be a visible contender than an invisible champion.

A Perfect Track Record

The Persona Principle is the only Image-Marketing formula that exploits this fundamental truth. The Persona Principle is a proven science. We have executed Persona Plans for all company sizes, from start-up to IBM. Persona has a perfect track record in building successful ventures on image alone. It recognizes that relying on basic truth is not enough.

This is not an exaggeration. This is not hype. The idea that image is more important than substance has been recognized since mankind became civilized. Even tribal societies wore trophies of their hunting conquests to show their prowess to other members of society. It is not enough to be the greatest hunter in the village. The entire village must know it.

In 1819, Washington Irving wrote, "In civilized life, where the happiness, and indeed almost the existence, of man depends so much on the opinion of his fellow man, he is constantly acting a studied part." The Persona Principle takes this concept to the ultimate conclusion. We have turned an intuitive art into a mathematical science. This science does not depend on trends or changing morals. It is based on two unchanging human truths:

★   Image has more value than reality.
★   To last, image must be built only on truths.

Persona Profile: The Lasting Image

It is not enough to be visible. To last is to succeed. And to last, Persona is the most effective weapon in your marketing war chest. The top five advertisers[3] have been leaders for decades:

#1 Brand: AT&T telephone

#2 Brand: Ford cars, trucks, and vans

#3 Brand: Kellogg's cereals

#4 Brand: Sears stores

#5 Brand: McDonald's restaurants

Not surprisingly, these brands lead in spending. But they started from modest beginnings—using many of the principles outlined in The Persona Principle—to become the giants of today. Although McDonald's spent $208,992,400 in 1994, this figure is only a small percentage of its extraordinary revenue. In fact, as a percentage of revenue, McDonald's spending is below average.

Spending may seem the main rule of success for these big brands, but of more importance is image. Even an exorbitant level of spending would not have built McDonald's into the number one fast-food chain without a clear and consistent persona. Without image—corporate culture, advertising character, restaurant decor, all of which must appeal to the specific target audience—no amount of spending would bring McDonald's to the top.

McDonald's controlled every ad and expenditure in marketing to maintain a consistent image. The McDonald's persona is the true secret to its success. Ronald McDonald and the Hamburglar have been so consistently promoted that they are a part of the North American culture. The credibility message "billions served" has been a cornerstone of McDonald's persona-building for decades. Such consistency of message and image is crucial to any persona success story.

All brand leaders have something in common: they all value long-term image. But how did they become these giants that practically every citizen of the United States and Canada knows by name? Without exception, Persona leaders had humbler beginnings. They followed the most important codes of the Persona Principle:

★ They invented or refined their product to be different from any similar product (see Persona Code 53, Code of Invention).

★ They made credible claims (see Persona Factor 4, the Credibility Factor).

★ They never compromised, treating their persona as an inviolable culture (see Persona Factor 5, the No-Compromise Factor).

★ They allowed their persona to become a distinct, almost living, entity, complete with unique characters, names, logos, and styles (see Persona Factor 8, the Independence Factor).

It is difficult for the average start-up entrepreneur to relate to these giants. Yet these were once small ventures. McDonald's began humbly as a single restaurant and then a handful of unknown restaurants. Finally, McDonald's was bought by a shrewd entrepreneur who developed the McDonald's culture. This culture became an empire.

Every code and factor of the Persona Principle is feasible, applicable by ventures of any size, whether young start-up or McDonald's. If you use the codes, your Image-Equity will grow (see Persona Factor 6, the Growth Factor). Your venture could become a McDonald's or a Kellogg's with steady, precise, uncompromising application of the Persona Principle.

The
Five Ages

▼

"It is only shallow people who do not judge by appearances.
The true mystery of the world is the visible, not the invisible."
Oscar Wilde

The Picture of Dorian Gray

Why is image so important in a world that is apparently moving away from core brands and wastefulness? Isn't it good enough just to be the best and wait for your prospects to come to you? Many Persona students ask these questions.

Persona strategy becomes crucially important in our changing world. We have analyzed five major trends in the world socio-economic structure that make Persona indispensable to your success. These trends will strongly affect the businesses of the future. They are important because of Persona Code 24, Code of Collective Conscious. Fighting trends will result in disastrous defeat. You must learn, appreciate, and use the trends of the next millennium.

Our new century will be defined by its trends. We can expect it to be characterized by the Five Ages.

The Age of Substance and Responsibility

Many marketers believe that the new age is all about "down-to-earth substance." While substance is important, the real issue is that companies must Persona-Position their images to appear more substantial—and socially responsible. The Persona Principle tells how to capitalize on this strong trend.

Consumers are redefining their own role. We no longer wish to be thought of as just consumers. We are now reusers, recyclers, and conservers. This movement of substance will gain momentum in the next century as populations grow and resources dwindle.
From a marketing perspective, it is not enough to be socially responsible. Your efforts must be visible. You must show your customers that you care.

Social marketing has become a vast specialty in marketing. New niche ad agencies that specialize in this field are growing faster than the big traditional agencies. Social marketing also impacts product development, packaging, and advertising. The minimum badge of acceptability is to print the recycled logo on packaging. Companies are no longer contributing to favorite charities for the tax benefits; instead, they are publicizing their commitment to society.

Consumers are demanding something for themselves as well. Not only do they want social responsibility, they also want the genuine article. The Real McCoy has more meaning now than when it was coined decades ago by consumers who only wanted to buy the original oil pump invented by Mr. McCoy.

Persona Profile: The Genuine Article

Two major marketing solutions are gaining popularity in the so-called Age of Substance and Responsibility: no-name brands and the genuine brand.

The nineties became a decade of disillusionment for many. The recession, combined with decades of overly hyped brands, pushed society to demand both more value and higher quality. It's no longer adequate to offer one or the other.

Consumers now demand the genuine article at the best price. Genuine Chevrolet is the current positioning from the GM giant. Genuine Draft is the promise of Miller Beer. The Real Thing is Coca-Cola's famous badge. Jockey shorts are Genuine Jockey.

Consumers want substance, not hype. They are not impressed with a claim of "best" or "better." But they can be swayed by claims of "the real thing" if the message is proven. Many consumers are message weary and advertising resistant. Going back to the genuine roots builds a strong persona for future growth as we enter the Age of Substance and Responsibility.

The Age of Small and Home Business

Executives are retiring early. Layoffs are shaking up the middle class. Big business is struggling. People are starting home businesses and consultancies in unprecedented numbers. There is a strong movement toward the notion that "smaller is better."

According to a Market Facts poll in 1994, 9 percent of all workers have a home business. Of these, 16 percent use cellular phones, 7.4 percent use portable computers, 13.1 percent use beepers, and 6.7 percent use on-line computer services. The popularity of the home office and the home business is surging.

Many companies now use "virtual" technology to build their images. Many wealthy entrepreneurs are working from a cottage or bedroom. In between changing diapers and walking the dog, they write proposals on their home computers. They fax their proposals with their modems and teleconference to close deals. Business people are communicating and marketing on the Internet and other on-line systems. The boardroom is now the computer. Video conferencing will soon replace the face-to-face meeting. Geography is no longer a barrier.

The persona potential of the virtual office is spectacular. The prospective client never sees your office, your clothes, your unwashed hair, or your informal home office. An international conglomerate can be run from your cottage. A sales professional can work from a car. The perceptions are controlled by the home business professional.

The advent of virtual technology, computers, and the Age of Small and Home Business presents a perfect opportunity for building controlled personas.

The Age of Confusion

The 1990s have seen the most momentous social changes since the Second World War. The marketing strategy of the eighties can be summarized as "let everyone know, and they'll come." The consumerism of the eighties has given way through recession to the conservatism of the nineties. Trends that used to be measured in years are now changing monthly. We are bombarded with a statistical average of 577 advertisements each working week—and typically we recall less than one percent. In this decade of confusion, maximizing impact and persona are crucial success requirements in marketing. Penetrating the jungle of messages can only be achieved three ways:

★   Using high-impact graphics and messages: this method will get you noticed but has no long-term value, since recall is linked statistically to frequency of advertising.
★   Using high-frequency advertising: this method will build recall and top of mind in your audience but has no value if the message and image change frequently.
★   Building a rock-solid persona: the value of your persona will

grow at a compound rate, reducing the need for costly advertising and "scream till you are noticed" techniques.

Persona becomes vitally important in the Age of Confusion. Extensive reach in advertising is now very difficult. The big television networks can no longer promise that they can reach all of America. The dozen-channel universe gave way to the 50-channel universe. The latest promise from the cable industry is the 500-channel universe. New technologies such as satellite systems, compression signals, and fiber optics will bring these hundreds of channels to most of America within a handful of years.

Advertisers have no easy way to reach their prospects. Consumers are weary of message bombardment, which only promises to become more cluttered. The opportunities for building strong brand images—the Levi's jeans and the Duracells of the future—are limited. Advertisers cannot reach their audience without spending a larger share of their revenue. As the media change rapidly, companies that do not change to a Persona strategy (to maximize equity) will find themselves spending much more to achieve far less. Some companies are still resorting to marketing warfare by bombardment, spending immense sums of money to reach as many as possible. Others are using selective guerrilla warfare, placing snipers in the trees to pick off consumers with clever offers.

Both of these strategies will fail without a strong persona. The mass confusion of messages makes recall among consumers difficult to achieve, even through bombardment. Only the consistency of a strategic persona can improve recall.

Impact is becoming increasingly more important. Many advertisers carry this belief to incredible extremes. Every Super Bowl brings another extravaganza of special effects advertising. The combined reach and high impact have resulted in recall; however, this expensive strategy is beyond the reach of most companies.

Impact can be as simple as being different (see Persona Code 27, Code of Impact.) Instead of copying the success of a competitor—a standard practice in beer advertising—the Persona practitioner stands out with its own differentiated image.

Persona Profile: The Beer Wars

Nowhere in the marketing universe is the Age of Confusion more evident than in the endless beer wars. Beer companies spend more on individual brand advertising than any other segment of the consumer product industry. Budweiser spent $117 million reaching its audience. Miller almost matched it at $105 million. The cost of reaching this audience is constantly increasing as consumers tune in to many choices of media. Budweiser increased spending on media by 28 percent between 1994 and 1995. Not surprisingly to us, revenues have not climbed by a corresponding amount.

Increased spending is not the answer in the beer wars. The breweries must redefine and reinforce their personas, because there is so little difference among the personas of these megabreweries that recall scores are low on all beer brands, despite spending on high-reach advertising.

In Canada, the struggle for attention in the beer wars took a nasty turn. Labatt Brewery launched its heavily advertised "Genuine" cold-filtered draft weeks before Miller "Genuine" cold-filtered reached Canada from the United States (through Molson breweries). Even though Miller was the originator of the technology, Labatt was first into the market, capturing much of the attention. Molson fought back by producing a series of aggressive full-page ads that accused Labatt of copying its technology and even its packaging and name. Labatt had successfully grabbed all the Image-Equity in cold-filtered beer before Miller could reach Canada, but Molson fought back with ads that could not be ignored by the beer-drinking public.

What resulted from the ensuing publicity in the beer wars was that both brands received major attention—breaking through the confusion barrier. Lawsuits and counter-lawsuits brought headlines. Cold-filtered was the only beer segment to grow in 1992.

Into this melee entered Canada's well-known "no-name king," Dave Nichol, originator of the private label President's Choice. Dave is a master of persona. He succeeded in building his no-name label to the level of a brand. President's Choice had become synonymous with both quality and value.

Dave had built such strong equity in his nonbrand that he entered the beer wars with confidence. Using Persona techniques, he differentiated his product. He asked his developers what ingredients made a superior beer. To separate his product from the competition (see Persona Code 53, Code of Invention) he used only the most expensive Saaz hops—even though the premium hops cost ten times more than the cheaper ones. Then he insisted his beer be aged one week longer than any other premium.

Borrowing on strong Image-Equity from his President's Choice brand, he launched a superior beer—PC Premium Draft—at a lower price. This carefully plotted approach is consistent with the image strategy of all of President's Choice brands: providing the best quality at the lowest price (see Persona Code 20, Code of Continuity).

The reaction from the giant breweries was instantaneous. Molson introduced new Valu-Packs to help compete against the private label. Unable to keep the no-name beer in stock, PC Premium Draft sold out.

In a brilliant guerrilla-marketing tactic, Dave executed Persona Code 3, Code of Playing Hard to Get. Full-page ads appeared across Canada with the headline: "Sorry, Dave Nichol!! We let you down!! We never expected the kind of demand your beer has generated!!" This ad from the brewer promised that beer lovers would have to wait only a few weeks for new supplies. This incredible Persona technique produced the intended results, and PC Premium Draft became a major contender in the beer wars.

The Death of the Brand Name

The advertising industry is prematurely mourning the passing of the brand. The onslaught of private labels and the struggles of mammoth brands to survive make the demise of the big brands seem imminent.

However, no-name and private-label brands are, in fact, clever persona brands. No-names are brand names that are Persona-Positioned to appear to be nonbrands that appeal to the value-conscious. The private-label phenomenon became powerful in the last recession. The emergence of the Age of Substance and Responsibility quickly turned this phenomenon from a potential fad into a long-term branding strategy.

The designations *no-name* and *private label* conjure up images of plain packaging and lower prices. Store chains all over North America are capitalizing on the Image-Equity built into these words. Some no-names have evolved into sub-brands.

Private labels have become permanent and growing marketing brands. These labels have developed personas that consistently suggest value, and quality, and substance through avoidance of excessive or elaborate packaging. The Age of Substance and Responsibility has made the private label movement one of the rapid growth strategies of Image-Marketing.

Persona Profile: No-Name Branding

Some no-name brands borrow equity from established brands by virtually copying the leaders. Vaseline Intensive Care's packaging was copied right down to the shape and colors by a private brand called Skin Care Lotion. Pepto-Bismol's famous pink bottle with dispenser cap was copied by Relief Plus. Although borrowing equity may work short term (and probably will result in lawsuits), private label has its own equity. Dave Nichol used the Persona Code of the Package to develop the bland yellow no-name label that became so popular in Canada. Rather than borrow from the Image-Equity of established brands, most no-name strategists use the Persona Code of the Package technique, making their packaging look inexpensive and socially responsible to attract value-conscious shoppers.

No-name strategy employs eleven different Persona Codes to build Image-Equity. So much equity is invested in the no-name brand—the cumulative power of hundreds of no-names—that bigger brands are struggling.

Even areas such as health products are assailed by private labels. Sales of "Genuine" Bayer pain reliever products dropped 17 percent in 1994, compared to those of the previous year. That same year, the market share of private-label aspirins grew 6 percent.

In frozen potato products, private labels are number two, after Ore-Ida but ahead of McCain. In frozen vegetables, private labels are number one, with a 37.6 percent market share in 1994.

Private labels are winning in many categories and growing in others. No-name truly is the brand of the Age of Substance and Responsibility.

The Age of Self-Help

The proliferation of self-help books, the firing of ad agencies by the big advertisers (too many handlers, too many secrets, not enough strategic marketing), and the surge of growth in consultancies all signal the Age of Self-Help.

Self-help is not a new phenomenon, but it has grown in popularity in the jaded early nineties. Marketers are no longer godlike gurus to be worshiped or obeyed. Consultants are now just experts with an opinion. The ultimate decisions are being made through self-help techniques such as the Persona Principle.

In the early nineties, dozens of big advertising agencies folded. Thousands of advertising agency members were put out of work. This downsizing paralleled what was happening with the agencies' clients: reorganization, horizontal management rebuilding, and cost-cutting. The handlers were the first to go. The account execs and managers, who were go-betweens, were slashed. The client wanted direct access to the strategic and creative teams.

The self-help phenomenon is not limited to small companies or entrepreneurs on tight budgets. Large corporations are investing in training, such as Persona workshops, to improve the internal skills of their employees, depending less and less on outside experts. Persona is the first complete self-help marketing system that takes the nonexpert through all the scientific steps of strategic Image-Marketing. Agencies and consultants are no longer being asked to do everything. The clients are in control, creating their own personas, building their own Persona Plans, with consultants hired only to execute specific areas of the plan that require an expert. A majority of clients still employ full-service consultants, but the client is more knowledgeable and fully in control. Self-help is all about self-control.

PART TWO

THE FIVE POWER PERSONAS

▼

*"Play out the game, act well your part,
and if the gods have blundered, we will not."*
Ralph Waldo Emerson
Journals

The Extremes of Persona

▼

"There is a homely adage which runs: Speak softly and carry a big stick; you will go far."
Theodore Roosevelt

The five Power Personas are the most unbalanced but powerful extremes of the Persona Principle. Some "speak softly"—and some do not—but all Power Personas "carry a big stick." Although we advocate creating your own customized and balanced persona (see Part 5, A Persona How-To), learning the Five Power Personas will give you ammunition and guidelines that can be incorporated in your own persona.

Pure Power Personas are rare and very difficult to achieve. Only one Power Persona can exist in a specific industry. Most pure Power Personas should be avoided by Image-Marketers. The major Power Personas are presented here only to demonstrate the extremes of Persona.

You will construct your own Persona Plan based on an in-depth Persona Inventory. The resulting plan will determine your persona. You may deliberately choose to incorporate aspects of one of these Power Personas to give your venture teeth, but only as tools to achieve your specific, customized objectives.

Emperor Persona

The Emperor Persona is the most overt and obnoxious of the Five Power Personas. It is the one most often adopted by history's military dictators. The most important element in creating an Emperor Persona is eliminating any visible signs of weakness.

Napoleon and Alexander the Great developed Emperor Personas. Napoleon, the diminutive soldier, became the Emperor through his version of Persona development.

The problem with Emperor Persona is that the arrogance of the image can and probably will eventually lead to a downfall. IBM, once the Emperor of computers, is fending off serious attacks to its Image-Equity from Compaq, Sun, Apple, Dell, and private labels. To survive, the Emperor is restructuring its persona as an Expert Persona.

Emperor Personas employ monopolistic approaches that can never last long. Even the once seemingly unassailable telephone monopolies have collapsed, leaving most large telecommunication companies in the position of having to reorganize their personas. Most Emperors opt to evolve into Expert Personas.

It is rarely recommended that new ventures develop a true Emperor Persona; however, certain elements of this persona can be incorporated into your customized Persona Plan. You should only consider a full Emperor Persona if:

★ You or your firm are considered to be market leader in your segment by a wide margin.
★ You have been the leader for many years.
★ You invented your segment or product and others copied you (this must be a known or visible fact, not a historical oddity).
★ You are highly respected as the best in your segment in quality or price or both.
★ You are a gambler.
★ You are arrogant.
★ You love yourself and your venture.

The last three requirements are not meant to be humorous. If you do not completely love yourself and your product with absolute and unabated conceit, you will never become the Emperor. The Emperor must believe unconditionally in his venture.

The characteristics of the Emperor Persona are:
★ Arrogant confidence in his leadership.
★ Dictatorial management style.
★ Aggressive response to any intruders in his territory.
★ Use of mainstream marketing methods.
★ Susceptibility to marketing guerrilla attacks because of cumbersome management structures.
★ Number one position in his segment, averaging double the sales of the main competitor.
★ Instant propaganda response to any negative public relations.
★ Hiding of all public weaknesses.
★ Occasional descents from the dais to visit with subjects for rare and heavily publicized events.

Persona Profile: Long Live the Emperors
The Emperor Persona requires stature. According to *Advertising Age* magazine, the "names with the greatest cachet" are:
★ Coca-Cola
★ Kodak
★ Sony
★ Mercedes-Benz

Other important Emperors include Disney and Levi's jeans. These companies share one thing in common: their unshakable belief in their own culture and image. All have dozens of competitors but remain kings of their categories. The arrogance has softened with major encroachments from companies such as Pepsi and Lexus, but Coca-Cola and Mercedes-Benz remain the Emperors through consistent and aggressive application of Persona Imaging.

Hero Persona

The Hero Persona builds its success base on the skills of one hero. Ad agencies and law firms usually build their companies on the reputation of their hero. Instead of building the image of the company to the stature of Emperor, the Hero Persona invests in the leader or nominal leader of the venture. For example, Ford automobiles were built according to the vision of Henry Ford.

The Hero can be brought in as a token partner, to be the public front man. More often, the Hero Persona venture will promote its real heroes. Law firms make sure their key partners are featured in the firm's name. Ad agencies such as Ogilvy & Mather, J. Walter Thompson, or Leo Burnett use similar strategies.

You might consider a Hero Persona if:
★   You are acknowledged to be the very best in your field (it is not enough to be the best; you must be acknowledged).
★   You can partner with someone who is the very best in your field.
★   You can patiently cultivate hero status by trading your considerable expertise for public acclaim (this is essentially marketing the hero).
★   You are conceited and like to see your name everywhere.

Don't let your personal quest for fame force you down the path of Hero Persona. Remember that you must be the best and then be acknowledged to be the best. Otherwise, consider developing the Expert Persona.

The hero must be appealing. Negative heroes don't work. The hero must either be famous or become famous to have any value.

The other characteristics of the Hero Persona are:

★ Company bears the name of the hero.
★ Hero must be above reproach and cannot have a private life.
★ Hero must be perfect in the eyes of the public.
★ Company revolves around the hero center, even if the hero is no longer with the company (remember Colonel Sanders?).
★ Hero ventures must avoid scandals at all cost.
★ Hero does not actually have to be the true leader of the venture, but should appear to be.

Persona Profile: The Name Hero

The name of a hero can be enough to build a world business. Three of the biggest names in the entertainment business— Steven Spielberg, Jeffrey Katzenberg, and David Geffen—formed their own film and record company, Dreamworks SKG, in 1995. With the weight of these big heroes, their success is virtually guaranteed. They will emerge with a new venture that will require very little marketing.

One of the key advantages of the Hero Persona is the equity of the hero's name. Steven Spielberg carries billions of dollars in equity in his name alone. Finding a hero of stature can be expensive, but it can be a powerful weapon in the image wars. Success will be measured by the stature of the hero.

Expert Persona

The Expert Persona is far more modest than the Hero. The Expert Persona venture directs all marketing at building credentials, collecting them as a stamp collector hoards stamps. The Expert Persona subtly presents his credentials everywhere, ensuring credibility. This is a valuable persona for professionals, especially lawyers and doctors, who are restricted by laws that govern their advertising. But the Expert Persona is valuable in almost any service-oriented sector. The false modesty of the expert is more appealing to consumers than the arrogance of the Hero.

You might consider adopting the Expert Persona if:
★   You are already considered an expert in your field.
★   You have built a reputation within a well-established firm and wish to "go it on your own."
★   You can partner with someone who is considered an expert.
★   You can take your considerable experience and market yourself to reach acknowledged expert status (in other words, take your invisible credits and make them very visible).

The characteristics of the Expert Persona are:
★   Complete confidence in the product or service offered.
★   Vast knowledge in the segment.
★   Ranking in the top three of the field in expertise.
★   A natural expertise that's fully contained in the memory (crib notes are not allowed to experts).
★   Confidence in public and enjoyment of the spotlight, along with a healthy conceit dosed with crafted modesty.
★   Likability and/or respectability.
★   Invention of the segment by the expert or modification of the product to differentiate it from the competition.

Persona Profile: The Body Shop

The Body Shop was not named for founder and expert Anita Roddick, but the company rides on her very capable shoulders. Anita grew her company on her own respectable image and solid principles. Her company has grown to earn $666 million in sales in 1993—without spending a cent on advertising. Her success was based on an image-only Persona strategy.

The Body Shop *is* Anita Roddick. Her exploits as she traveled Africa and Asia in search of natural secrets are the stuff of consumer legend. Her customers know her commitment to social causes. Anita and the Body Shop stand for two main principles of: a new method of production not based on animal testing and providing aid to developing countries. Most of Anita's clients share her genuine concern for the environment. They purchase her natural products and either reuse or recycle the packaging.

Anita's image is integral to The Body Shop. Her expertise—and her commitment to social issues—is expected in her products.

Buddy Persona

The Buddy Persona is one of the most flexible of all the Power Personas. This is everyone's friend who treats everyone equally and is respected by everyone. The Buddy Persona is popular with the later generations of politicians and the new breed of corporate executive who can no longer afford to be ruthless and unapproachable. The truth is that these buddies are very unapproachable, but they are very capable actors who inspire confidence through carefully crafted routines. They appear to be your friend—but only to achieve their objectives.

The corporate penthouse executive is a vanishing breed. The horizontal corporation is fast becoming the reality of corporate culture. To defend the power of their positions, many Emperor Persona executives are recasting their images to follow the Buddy Persona. They now use sympathy, smiles, rationales to accomplish what they used to execute on a whim.

Many corporations have hybrid Buddy Personas. The next time you see a sweet-talking ad that sways you with good old-fashioned down-home common sense, you are being sold to by the most influential of personas—the Buddy. The Buddy has a unique ability to sell to almost anyone. Buddies are more sophisticated than the stereotyped salesperson, but their techniques are basically the same: convince with reason, overcome objections, and close.

The Buddy Persona is a powerful weapon for the late nineties, but only in sophisticated hands. The Buddy can appear insincere and almost ludicrous when poorly executed. But a master Buddy can sell anything reasonable to any reasonable person.

You might consider adopting the Buddy Persona if:
★ You are a natural-born salesperson (there is such a thing as a natural-born salesperson!).
★ You are able to impart a sales culture to your venture.
★ You genuinely like people but do not get emotionally involved with your audience.
★ You are an Emperor Persona now and are finding this image unappealing to your cynical or value-conscious prospects.
★ Your venture is very open with the audience, and those in the leadership have extroverted personalities.

The characteristics of the Buddy Persona are:
★ A warm and ostensibly caring surface that hides a cool and calculating strategy.
★ An appearance of being socially responsible by following current trends such as use of recycled papers and bare-bones packaging.
★ A flexible attitude to customer service, including responsiveness to complaints.
★ A reassuring guarantee or promise.
★ Token or genuine efforts to support local community activities.

Simpatico Persona

The cause-oriented Simpatico Persona is the persona of choice with business and political evangelists. The power of Simpatico lies in the flexible character technique. The evangelist sells his cause at every opportunity by modifying the pitch to be sympathetic with the audience receiving the message. The Simpatico Persona is also known as the Chameleon Persona.

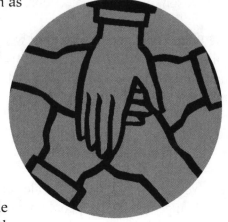

The Simpatico Persona is one of the most dynamic of the Power Personas. It demands religious fanaticism—a sense of real cause. The cause can be the goals of the company. Often the evangelism is limited to the extravagant culture of the company. Macintosh,[4] from Apple Computer, is a clear example of the Simpatico Persona. The brand Macintosh has a strong culture that is religiously maintained in all marketing strategies. Even the staff is indoctrinated with the elaborate corporate culture.

You might consider Simpatico Persona if:
★   You are a team-oriented venture with enthusiastic participants.
★   You are capable of living the created culture.
★   You believe absolutely in the benefits of your service or product.
★   You are evangelical about your cause.

The characteristics of Simpatico Persona are:
★   Genuine enthusiasm for the venture.
★   A total cultural environment within the venture.
★   A strong sense of cause (fund-raising ventures can benefit from Simpatico).
★   An audience-oriented culture that is flexible to the needs of clients.
★   A customer-service-oriented venture.

Persona Profile: The Macintosh Revolution

Perhaps the boldest and most effective Simpatico Persona ad of all time was the much acclaimed Apple Macintosh launch. Played only once during the Super Bowl in 1983, the visual extravaganza employed Ridley Scott's moody effects and Orwellian overtones, but it captured the imaginations of consumers so intensely that Macintosh was perceived as not just a product, but an entire culture—almost a religious cause. Macintosh promised the first user-friendly computer. This unique Simpatico approach was demonstrated in an image ad that was revolutionary in many ways.

A lone female athlete trashes the rigid Big Brother culture of DOS with a neatly thrown hammer. She is chased by guards into a room full of gray, identically dressed people watching an imposing image on a giant screen. The 1984 Big Brother on the screen is droning on endlessly about the unification of information systems.

Without a word she shatters the DOS world, destroying the giant screen with her hammer—a clearly revolutionary metaphor. The violence of the ad uses aggressive Simpatico to suggest that the era of big, cold computers is over, replaced by the era of the friendly computer. This is Simpatico for the DOS-weary audience. The headline flashes: "On January 24, Apple Computer will introduce Macintosh. And you'll see why 1984 won't be like *1984*."

The ad only played once, but it was never forgotten. Later Macintosh ads were friendlier, showing the warm characteristics of a Buddy Persona, but the evangelism of the Macintosh cause fully entrenched the powerful Simpatico Persona.

As original as the execution of this famous ad seems to be, all of the basic rules of Persona Imaging were incorporated. Apple Computer built a culture (The Image Factor) using high impact (Code of Impact) and reach (Code of Reach). Now considered one of the greatest ads of all time, the Macintosh launch was a classic Persona image launch. Apple used the Code of Singularity to separate Macintosh from the PC standard. They used the Code of the Hero (the athlete breaking the television screen) to create a counterculture that reacted against the DOS- dominated world. The company established instantly with one ad that it was the Simpatico Persona of computers. Within months, Apple was terrifying the blue suits at IBM.

The Custom Persona

The Power Personas are not suitable for most ventures. Each company and product should develop its own persona based on the Factors and Codes of Persona. This process can be either informal or formal.

The informal method involves reading this book, understanding the concepts, and developing your own system for developing a customized persona for your venture. We recommend you inventory all of your image assets and liabilities as described in Part 5 of this book. The formal method is a complex and complete system that uses a mathematical index to measure your venture against a standard. This method leads to a formal plan that prioritizes your steps to success.

Whichever method you choose, you will be surprised what you learn in the process. Many Persona students have come up with brilliant concepts in the middle of a Persona Inventory.

The first step in developing a customized persona for your venture is to study Parts 3 and 4 of this book. You should understand the 8 Persona Factors and 88 Persona Codes before beginning your Persona Plan.

PART THREE

THE 8 PERSONA FACTORS

▼

"There is an invisible garment woven around us from our earliest years; it is made of the way we eat, the way we walk, the way we greet people, woven of tastes and colors and perfumes which our senses spin...."
Jean Giraudoux
Siegfried

The Image
Factor

▼

The image of success has more value
than tangible success.

....

Definition

Brand marketers have known for years that the persona of a product
has more value than the substance. The persona must be based in
truth, but it must also be a strategically formulated image that appeals
to your specific audience—your potential clients.
If you look successful, people will assume you are. With this
perception, you gain confidence and credibility—the most important
elements in any relationship. You do not gain either
by being the best or having endless credentials. Your credentials must
become prominently visible to your prospects, or they
will gather dust.

....

What It Means

"It is easy to be beautiful; it is
difficult to appear so."
Frank O'Hara

Meditations in an Emergency

The first time we quoted this Persona Factor, years ago, it was to a new client. We projected a slide that said: "The Equity of your image is more important than your tangible assets." He almost stormed from the room. Needless to say, he disagreed most heartily. He eventually came around to our way of thinking, but only after we explained that his financial assets were also important—just not *as* important.

Your bank account, your assets, your building, your staff, your T-bills, and your investments are all very important and valuable. Our seemingly controversial statement does not make light of any of these elements. It merely states that the success of any venture can benefit more from the equity of image than from the money invested in it.

Millions of dollars have been poured into losing ventures in the past. As history has shown us, nearly bankrupt companies are not always saved by massive infusions of cash. Any company that is noticeably losing money has more than financial woes—it has a major image problem. Even if its problems were caused by mismanagement and poor investing, the confidence of stakeholders will not return until an image that inspires confidence is reestablished.

A start-up venture has no equity value. Venture capitalists are hesitant to pour their millions into companies that promise only a great idea. They look for a solid, unique angle—an image—before investing. Banks do not underwrite business loans without business plans that paint a complete picture of the venture: image, capabilities of staff, financial assets, and marketing plans.

Image is always first and most important. Truth is second. Credibility is third. Money is at best fourth in value, whether we're talking about a start-up or established business.

But building an image is not as simple as just becoming visible. To create a successful image, you must become visible with a carefully crafted persona. Your persona will be based on truth, be credible, and be customized to your audience. Each of the Persona Factors in this section of the book deals with the most important aspects of your persona: image, truth, customization, credibility, a no-compromise philosophy, growth, research and independence. Of these, image is the most important. The image is the first aspect of Persona to which your target audience is exposed.

A plumber's image of success is different from a banker's. An accountant's image is the opposite of an artist's. You can customize your image to your industry and your audience using the 8 Persona Factors.

Here's how it works: your core truth comes first. In other words, what you offer is paramount. *How* you offer it comes next. To accomplish this step, you must study your audience and learn what it responds to. Establishing credibility is a long process, and you must follow a clear-cut strategy for building believability in your persona. You must never compromise your persona for any reason. If you follow all these steps, your persona will grow on its own until your venture is completely independent of its creators.

It all starts with an image that makes you as visible as possible to those who could buy into your offering. Never stop telling your audience you are the best, and make sure that everything you do and say reflects your image as number one. With persistence, the status you claim will become accepted truth.

Image Factoring Techniques
There are six keys to a successful image:
*   Image must be anchored in truth.
*   Your projected image must be unique and differentiating.
*   Never stop reaching your audience with your image.
*   Only show those aspects of your image that support your persona.
*   Never show weaknesses.
*   Conduct a complete image Audit by executing a formal or informal Persona Inventory.

The Story of Jerry Hind
For eight years, Jerry Hind tried to close the annual $2 million contract with Western Ducting. Every year he bid. Every year he lost.

Jerry was friendly with Henry Malone, vice president at Western, but the contract always went to Jerry's main competitor. Jerry phoned Henry weekly, sent him postcards from wherever he went, never forgot a Christmas gift, and even got to know Henry's family. He joined Henry's club and always let him win at tennis.

Jerry was frustrated because he knew that his company was better and more competitive than the firm that was selected each year. After three years—exasperated by his lack of success—Jerry cornered Henry at lunch and asked him why he never won the contract.

Jerry didn't like the answer. Henry told him that the contract was too big to give to a friend. He said that the stakes were too high to trust a small company. Angry, Jerry demanded to know why Henry thought they couldn't handle the deal. He was shocked by the answer. Henry commented on their small, inaccessible office and even on Jerry's taste in clothes and cars.

Jerry limped home to his nice suburban postwar bungalow in Scarborough. He told his wife the whole story, hugged his kids, and didn't sleep all night. He sat at his desk and thought about all the deals he had won and lost. By morning, he had made a risky decision.

Jerry went out and leased a brand-new Mercedes with payments he couldn't afford. He also bought an Armani suit—with the last of his savings. He stopped inviting clients to his company's simple office and made sure all his prospects saw his shiny white Mercedes. He stopped wearing the inexpensive watch his daughter had given him, even though he couldn't afford a better one. He also stopped going to Henry's club.

Six weeks later he closed a half-million-dollar deal with Air Conditioning Systems United and renewed a long-term contract with an old client. Client attitudes started to change.

It wasn't until six months later that Henry called Jerry and asked why he hadn't been to the club. Jerry spoke in a voice that was friendly but nonchalant as he told him he was too busy closing a big deal in Boston. He even turned down an invitation to play tennis. Jerry knew that Henry felt something important had changed. Three weeks later, while back in Boston closing a deal on a referral, he sent a postcard to Henry: *Sorry about the tennis. I really was busy. But how about next Tuesday? Best, Jerry.*

Jerry showed up at the club in his Mercedes. He was wearing a designer shirt and had a fresh haircut. He knew Henry was always prompt, so he arrived early and sat in the main driveway of the club with his engine idling. Five minutes later, Henry pulled in. Jerry opened the door of his new car as if he were just arriving and handed a twenty to the valet, making sure Henry saw him.

Jerry still let Henry win at tennis, but every time Henry asked him about business, he just smiled and changed the subject. Over the next month, they played only two more games. Finally, two weeks later, Henry told Jerry he was giving him the contract.

Jerry remained calm—until he got home. As soon as he closed his front door, he jumped up and down and hooted until his wife thought about calling the police. His new Persona image and Persona technique of playing hard to get had won the biggest contract of his career—with more than enough commission to pay for his expensive new car.

Persona Profile: The Nike Legend

Every year they try. Every year they fail. Reebok International has
been aggressively trying to push Nike from the image throne for
three years. Its goal was to be number one by 1995. Nike spent
$250 million to remain the legend, while Reebok took a big jump to
$100 million and third-place Adidas spent $210 million. Nike was
still the reigning king.

As is obvious, the spending-versus-revenue ratios indicate no
direct relationship between advertising spending and stature.
Adidas almost matched Nike's spending but remained below both
Nike and Reebok in revenues. In 1995, Nike's sales rose to $3.87
billion. Reebok and Adidas enjoyed $2.8 and $2.13 billion in sales.
While Adidas's spending almost equals that of Nike, its revenues
are only 60 percent those of the image giant. If spending were all it
takes, we would expect Adidas to be at least in second place
and climbing.

Nike is the image athletic shoe. In the beginning, Nike was not an
international giant. When it was still an unknown company, its
famous "swoosh" logo was created by a design student for a token
fee. The famous logo has become so valuable to Nike that the
happy student received shares in the now giant company for her
image-contribution—years after she created the symbol. And TV
spots now feature the Nike swoosh without even the name to
identify it. This example demonstrates the true power of
Persona. Even if Nike reduced ad spending, it would likely remain
the leader.

An Exercise in Image Factoring

Image Factoring can take many forms: the clothes you wear, the sign you hang, the stationery you design, even the way you answer the phone. To envision the importance of every element—small or large—examine the three logos below. Without looking at the synopsis of each of the following companies, match these descriptions to the logos:

Logo #1

Logo #2

Logo #3

* ★ Technology company is Logo # _____
* ★ Corporate services company is Logo # _____
* ★ Charity is Logo # _____

All of these Two Dimensions–created logos were produced from Persona Plans developed by the authors. All logos have successfully launched or repositioned the companies involved.

A logo is often the first thing your prospect will see. It is certainly the most consistent element of your image that they will be exposed to. In many cases, a logo can make or break a company. To see how accurate your impressions of these companies were, review these summaries of the above companies:

* ★ Logo #1 is the corporate logo of CCNS—The Information Place. CCNS is Canada's largest public information service providing services to thousands of lawyers, accountants, car dealerships and all the major banks. They decided to revitalize their logo as part of a formal Persona Plan. The rigid, all-inclusive format of the Persona Inventory led them to discover their own positioning statement. The Persona Inventory demands a three word or less description of the venture. They came up with "The Information Place," which they liked so much they tagged their company name and logo with the statement.

* ★ Logo #2 was created for the first World Autism Conference. The Autism Society of Canada, a charity dedicated to the needs of children with autism and their families, required a thematic look for the event to give it credibility worldwide. The event was hugely successful with attendees from dozens of countries. Many large charities incorporate logos into their personas because they need credibility to function.

* ★ Logo #3 is a logo for one of North America's largest cable companies, Regional Cable TV. Regional Cable TV, which had been operating under six different names and logos, was unified under one name and logo.

Persona Tip for Business

The most important investment you can make in business is in your
logo or word mark. In business, your logo is the first thing your
prospects will see—on your letterhead, in your ads, on your signs—
and it will set the tone of your entire company. If you cannot budget
the best logo possible, don't compromise (see Persona Factor 5, the
No-Compromise Factor). Have a word mark designed that fits your
Persona, and transform the word mark into a logo at a later date. If
you have an existing logo that doesn't seem to be working, combine
repositioning of your company with a new logo to produce the biggest
marketing event in your company history.

Persona Tip for Entrepreneurs

Entrepreneurs have the advantage of control. They are aggressive and
energetic. The biggest mistake entrepreneurs make is allowing their
own strong personality to form the Persona of the company. Even
though entrepreneurs most often form principle-driven companies, the
only time it is acceptable for entrepreneurs to inject their own
personality into the firm is if they are forming a Hero Persona or
Expert Persona (see Part 2: The Five Power Personas).

Persona Tip for Salespeople

Most salespeople represent a company with an established image.
The best strategy is to develop a "sales persona" that will portray a
success image and credibility while not contradicting the image of the
company. Never allow the weak areas of your company to be
revealed. If your company environment is unattractive, always meet
clients in their office. If your car is a junker, make sure your
prospective clients never see it. If you cannot afford a good watch,

take it off. Wear only the best clothes you can, even if it means buying only one nice outfit and dry-cleaning it often.

Persona Tip for Employees

Promoting yourself at work is very similar to marketing a company. All of the same principles apply. Be noticed. Project a specific persona designed to achieve your objective. If you want a promotion, determine what your employer requires of the person in that position—and then do everything conceivable to demonstrate that you have these qualities. Wear the right clothes. Say the right things. Make sure you're seen arriving early and staying late. Don't take lunches. Build yourself up to be valuable and indispensable— playing up only to those who can advance your career. Be careful, however, not to overdo the "kissing up to the boss" portion of the plan. Play a little hard to get to demonstrate that you are valuable.

Personal Persona Tip

Persona can be even more powerful in your personal life than in your business. Building a persona can make a seemingly unattractive person striking. Find your unique strengths, build a Persona Plan that is entirely your own, and show the world how beautiful your differences are. Wear clothes that draw attention to your strong points and hide your weaknesses. Image is as important in attracting the right people to your social circle as it is in attracting the right prospect for business. Whether you are trying to impress the neighbors, chair a local church drive, or just meet a new friend, use all of the image-building techniques of the Persona Principle, and your objectives can be achieved.

The Reality Factor

▼

Your image must be based on a truth.

Definition

Even though "the image of success has more value than real success," your image must be built on a solid foundation of truth. No brand can survive beyond the first purchase and no relationship can survive past the first meeting, if there is no substance behind the image.

What It Means

"Facts as facts do not always create a spirit of reality."
G. K. Chesterton

Come To Think of It

THE PERSONA **69** PRINCIPLE

Behind all images there must be a core of truth. McDonald's does not have to sell the best-tasting hamburger to be the most popular fast-food restaurant in the world. Indeed, McDonald's does not claim to have the best-tasting hamburger. The company's culture is based on three specific and true offerings: speed, fun, and value.

Truth is the most important foundation of the Persona Principle. Without truth a persona will collapse. Quality can not be a whimsical concept. You may be able to convince your prospect to try you once based on your image promise, but it won't happen a second time unless you have the quality to back your claims.

Without knowing your strengths—and equally important, your weaknesses—you cannot build an image based on truths that are meaningful to your audience. Without truth you cannot build credibility. Without credibility, your image is worthless.

Reality Factoring Techniques

You must find your unique truth. Every venture or person can claim to be the best at something. Find your truth first, then find a way to make people believe it. To use Reality Factoring, it is important to follow these tips:

★ Never claim the same truth as an established competitor, even if you are better.
★ Study your audience and understand the truths they value.
★ Inventory all your truths.
★ Abandon those truths that do not seem credible.
★ Tone down any truths that are hard to prove and do not emphasize any truth that cannot be proved in five words.

The Story of Susan Pauling

Entrepreneur Susan Pauling built her company over nine hard years. Her public relations firm had enjoyed occasional successes. She made a decent living.

But Susan saw her associates out maneuvering her firm on every major pitch. She was rarely short-listed by the big clients. When she asked why she was not considered, the answer was always something like, "We like your work, but it's not what we're looking for."

Knowing she needed a revitalized image but uncertain about what she should do strategically, Susan moved her office to a shiny glass office tower on Bay Street in Toronto. She committed her company's liquid cash reserve to decorating her magnificent new office. She purchased expensive furniture, including a boardroom table that cost the company more than $20,000.

Susan's revenues plummeted. Her attempt to rebuild her image had failed. Her prospects did not buy into her success image.

Susan's future was not very promising. The economy was entering a business-wrecking recession and her business was grinding to a staggering halt. She needed help. In moving her office to prestigious Bay Street, Susan had understood the first Persona Factor, which dictates that "the image of success has more value than tangible success," but she had forgotten the second, which says "your image must be based on a truth."

Susan's family and friends got together at a Chinese restaurant to discuss the problem. Susan even invited her only two long-term clients. She polled them. She wrote down everything they told her. Then, she turned this information into a Persona Inventory that changed her company.

Susan had invested hundreds of thousands of dollars promoting her public relations firm over the last few years. She was hesitant to change directions at this point. If she did, she would blow any equity she had in her company. Unfortunately, her Persona Plan indicated that she had not differentiated herself from her aggressive competitors. Meanwhile, her Persona Inventory suggested that she had special talents working with corporate sponsors for public events. A quick review of the competition revealed that no one else was specializing in this area.

Susan's next step took real grit. She closed the doors to her public relations firm forever. The same day, she opened Pauling Entertainment. She retained her office and staff, changed her logo, and announced her specialty. She no longer did public relations work; instead, she brokered sponsors for entertainment or cultural industries. She connected corporate money with art galleries. She arranged sponsorships of sporting events. She went from an insignificant player in the public relations industry to the number one sponsor-broker in Canada. She became number one because hers was the only firm specializing in this growing field of marketing. And she was good at it, because in her public relations business she had arranged many sponsored events.

Susan's staff and office remained the same. The office decor was retained. The talents and skills of the staff were unchanged. She merely repositioned her persona to reflect her core talent—her truth. She discovered her true persona identity.

Profile

Persona Profile: From Zero to Four in Four Years

When is a Lexus better than a Mercedes? When it climbs to number four spot in North American sales—ahead of Mercedes, Volvo, BMW, Jaguar and Saab—on the top-ten luxury car hit parade. And the company did it in just four short years!

Lexus employed a Persona strategy to perfection. Toyota entered the luxury car market at a time when the recession was forcing most consumers to practice moderation. In an ingenious launch, Lexus challenged the seemingly insurmountable luxury status of Mercedes and BMW, achieving a 10.6 percent market share against Mercedes's 6.9 percent and BMW's 8.7 percent. How was this possible in just four years?

Persona demands that you discover your unique truth—your product's differentiated reality. Toyota was able to invent a new reality, since it was starting from scratch. It could have modeled itself after Cadillac: big, popular, and expensive, but rather weak on the quality standards. Or it could have copied the quality promise of Mercedes or the sportiness of BMW. However, any of these strategies would have doomed Toyota to failure.

Instead, Lexus swept into the luxury market with a promise of the highest possible quality at the lowest possible price. The Lexus LS 400 was an automobile equal in quality to a Mercedes but $10,000 lower in price. The carefully constructed Lexus persona was a magnificent success, and the brand leaped past the likes of Jaguar and BMW a short while after its launch. In name-recognition polls, Lexus is consistently in the top ten— beating out brands that have been around for decades.

The Lexus found a unique niche in the market, and Toyota's successful franchise produced a car that was voted number one for quality and satisfaction three years in a row by the well-known J. D. Powers consumer poll. We recognize that Lexus could not have enjoyed its ride to the top without the supporting reality of superb engineering. Consistently, in survey after survey, 98 percent of Lexus owners state that they will purchase another Lexus in future. This is more than a promise or an image—this is a reality.

An Exercise in Reality Factoring

In the recent movie *The Temp*, a charming temporary assistant with a sparkling image hoodwinks an entire office into believing she is destined for the vice presidency of the firm. Beneath her charming exterior image, however, is the heart of a psychopath. Eventually, her image breaks down as people realize that she is murdering the staff.

While this may be a somewhat heavy-handed example, it emphasizes that image without reality just doesn't work. Image is not a persona unless it is based on truth and credibility. No matter how carefully crafted, eventually image-only personalities must fail.

Study your venture. What are the five most important truths about your product or service? Now prove it in five words or less.

TRUTH	PROOF
1.	
2.	
3.	
4.	
5.	

How many of these truths are different from those offered by your main competitors?_____

★   If you have five truths that are different from those of your competitors—that you can prove in five words or less—you need no help from this factor. Just start building your image.

★   If you have two to four truths that are different, concentrate on forming your image around these healthy differences, ignoring completely the truths that are similar to those of the competition.

★   If you can offer only one truth that is different, you should start your Persona Inventory as soon as possible. Without some strongly defined differences you are going to fail.

★   If you can offer no truths beyond those of your competitors, you should skip right to Persona Code 53, Code of Invention.

Persona Tips for Business

Consumers have become wary of quality claims, so they expect poor service. The companies that set out to achieve excellence in quality control are the success stories of the nineties. Think about what it costs you if you lose a customer. For example, if your product is a consumable that retails for $25 and your customers typically buy eighteen of them a year, the loss of one customer will cost you $450 a year. If you are a consultant, the stakes are much higher, so that the loss of a customer could cost thousands.

To replace a lost customer, you may have to reach thousands of prospects. The cost of replacing a customer soon becomes higher than the loss of income. No business can afford to lose even one customer. If a customer demands a replacement, give it to her. If a client wants a written apology, you had better do more than write. But damage control is only a part of the solution. Preventing complaints through quality control will contribute more to your long-term success than any other technique.

Persona Tip for Entrepreneurs

Learn a lesson from Lexus. Before launching your venture, find an untouched niche that can be marketed meaningfully. Capitalize on the growing trend of "substance and responsibility." Instead of inventorying an existing venture, exploit the advantage of creating your own ideas from scratch. Don't miss the ideal opportunity this strategy presents. Launch a guerrilla-marketing war that will catch the entrenched competitors by surprise. Do the unexpected. Find a unique solution.

Persona Tip for Salespeople

It is important to learn the real substance, the true claim of your product. It is equally important that you study your own Persona to determine your root truth, your unique talents. Don't be a glad-hander who is comfortable making jokes with strangers; become the salesperson who is sincere and caring. Consumers are very intolerant of the aggressive salesperson. The hard-sell salesperson is a dinosaur of the consumerist sixties and seventies.

Consumers used to allow the hard sell to work because of their social politeness. They found it hard to say no or ignore the unwanted pitch. Every time we go to Mexico, we are astonished to see that the hard sell is still very much a way of life. On every street corner, outside every hotel, is a smiling salesperson who pounces the moment an unwary tourist leaves the safety of his resort. *"Holá, amigo!"* they shout enthusiastically. If you start to walk away, they chase you, still grinning. *"Amigo*, I have 50 percent off on rental Jeeps!" Are they rental-car salespeople? No! They are selling time-share condos! They made an extravagant offer to reel you in for their true pitch. But if you play spectator, you'll see the tourists looking away, walking faster, and avoiding the hard-sell salespeople.

Now that you realize that the hard sell doesn't work anymore, cultivate a sophisticated persona for your sales pitching that is equal to your company's persona. Build rationales for your prospects. Why should they buy what you are offering? As a salesperson, you are virtually an entrepreneur, so you must play by the same rules.

Persona Tips for Employees

How do you get ahead in workplaces that are laying off tenured employees and reorganizing horizontally, in a time when salaries are not growing and you are just plain lucky to have a job? Treat yourself as if you were a product being offered to consumers. Analyze your true strengths and weaknesses. Find new ways to be an asset to your company. Market yourself subtly at every opportunity, using all of the Persona Codes and Factors in this book.

Maintaining or advancing in the workplace is only slightly different from maintaining market share in a product category. Quality control, persona, and real skills are the tools for advancement. If you benefit your company, your company should reward you. If not, you can use the Persona techniques to market yourself to another company.

Personal Persona Tip

Personal Persona must also adhere to the sincere rules of substance. You may be able to construct a persona that allows you to meet that elusive someone, but if your persona is based on a lie, the relationship will not last. You must first discover the true you, the features and mannerisms that your friends love you for, then build these attributes into a truthful persona. If you are genuinely shy, do not try to built an extroverted persona. You may be noticed, but you will not be able to maintain the fraud. Be real, but weave a persona around your truths that enhances your appeal. If you are shy, build an elusive, secretive image. If you are extroverted, build a show-off persona. Customize your persona to your true identity.

The Custom Factor

▼

*Build a Persona based on your goal, then customize your
image based on your unique selling proposition.*

....

Definition
Although Persona must start with goals, the Custom Factor requires
that you customize and refine it to suit the unique nature of your
product, your target audience, and your personality. Without
uniqueness your persona cannot live.

....

What It Means
*"There is one quality more important than 'know-how.' This is 'know-what,'
by which we determine not only how to accomplish our purposes,
but what our purposes are to be."*
Norbert Wiener

The Human Use of Human Beings

Your goals will determine your route to success. You are not ready to build a persona until you have defined your specific goals. Once you have goals, you can map the route to your success.

You will study your prospective clients—those important people who will help you achieve your goals. You must understand your target audience's needs. What motivates your audience to buy your service? What benefit appeals to them? Only with this knowledge can you customize your persona to suit their needs. Don't make any fast assumptions about their needs. Research this issue carefully, and you will be able to customize your persona for maximum success. Remember, your goals are your targets; your audience's goals are your tools. And you need to have a clear vision of both.

Custom Factoring Techniques

The easiest way to customize your persona is to do a full Persona Inventory to determine your audience's preferences, your competition's persona, and your opportunities:

★ Take your core truth and add one word that makes it more appealing to your audience.

★ Describe your core truth in five different ways. Test each way of expressing your true claims by doing informal polling of your prospects.

★ If your truth is identical to your competition's—and you are not the leader in your market—find a new way to express this truth, or find a new truth to express.

★ Customize your claims to each sector of your audience and prepare a separate positioning statement for each of these specific prospect groups.

The Story of Jeff Krieff

Jeff Krieff's last meeting with his bank did not go well. He had barely stopped the bank from calling his loans. Meanwhile, they had frozen his operating line of credit. If Jeff had been a drinker, he would already be on his fourth drink. Instead, he sat at his desk, his head between his hands, trying to figure out where he had gone wrong. His company's Kritek Workstations were the best PCs on the market. They were fast Pentium computers that in every way matched or bettered the competition. Not only were they better, faster, and fully PC compatible, but they were also far less expensive than IBM, Compaq, and other systems.

What went wrong? Jeff sold quite a few units the first couple of years. He even lowered his prices as production increased. But then sales plummeted. The bank panicked. Jeff's headache became permanent. He had even committed a large percentage of revenues to advertising the Kritek, only to experience a complete lack of response, not even one call on his toll-free line.

Jeff called a meeting of his sales force and asked them what they thought the problem was. They reaffirmed the fact that the Kritek system was superior in technology and lower in price than the competition. Jeff probed them for customer comments, which revealed that all current Kritek customers were satisfied. The difficulty was in attracting new customers.

Jeff tried one more blitz of advertising, committing his reserve money. The ads offered a new, lowered price. He sold one system.

Reluctantly, Jeff began laying off his staff. His staff members were his friends and the duty was agonizing. The next meeting at his bank was equally painful. He was told that he must submit a complete business plan and marketing plan to the bank before the end of the month or face losing his credit.

Kritek was virtually bankrupt. Jeff had tried everything he could think of. Finally, in desperation, he called his old friend at IBM. Jeff had known Lynn for almost twenty years. They had worked together at IBM before Jeff had ventured out on his own. He bought her dinner, told her the whole sob story, and asked if she thought IBM would take him back. She actually laughed at him. Then she stung him with the truth. "You will never be able to compete for our customers. You have no brand awareness. All you have is a superior product. So what? No one knows it. And you certainly don't have the money to reach the end users."

Jeff didn't find her comment particularly helpful. But he listened to what she had to say. "You missed your marketplace. You're trying to sell to the wrong audience. Instead of selling to the end user—which is impossible with your limited resources—you should be selling to value-added resellers. There aren't so many of them to reach. All you have to do is offer them a great price."

Jeff almost spilled his coffee. It had never occurred to him to sell wholesale. The margins were in the direct-to-the-end-user sales. But the more he thought about it, reduced margins or not, the more logical it seemed. There were only thousands of VARs to reach, as opposed to millions of end users. His overhead wasn't high, so he could offer competitive pricing.

The next day he called his sales staff together and asked their opinion. They thought it was a terrible idea. But he persisted, explaining the logic to them. He charged them with compiling a list of all VARs and contacting all the magazines to which VARs subscribe. He had his production people work up a wholesale pricing schedule based on minimal markups.

Kritek Workstations remained invisible to the computer end user. But the company had not vanished. Within weeks, Kritek sales were skyrocketing, and the cash flowed in. VARs loved Kritek's low pricing and high quality. Jeff added telephone support for the VARs and extended his guarantees. He added the resellers' logos to his computer, hiding the Kritek badge. While Kritek seemingly disappeared to one audience, through customization of positioning it became the best-selling private-label computer.

Kritek revenues climbed 600 percent each year for three years. Jeff doubled his staff and added a staff profit-sharing plan. Quality, job satisfaction, and production increased. Kritek systems are now sold under more than a hundred different badges—none of them Kritek. But Jeff and his bank couldn't be happier. He had customized his offering to a specific target audience. The strategy had saved his company.

Persona Profile: Smartfood
Popcorn is peanuts in the megasized snack-food market dominated by Hostess and Frito-Lay. But Ken Meyers used classic guerrilla marketing to launch a snack customized for the premium snacker. Smartfood was introduced with no fanfare or advertising.

Simply appearing in stores, the expensive ready-made white-cheese popcorn was a smash hit from the first year. Sales in year one were a respectable $500,000, climbing to $18 million within four years.

The snack market is a brutal multimillion-dollar arena. New competitors are not easily tolerated by the giant snack-food companies, whose advertising budgets are typically in the millions for their popular products.

What Ken Meyers launched was a unique snack. He customized the persona of the snack, promoting the natural ingredients and distinctive white-cheese flavor. Ken employed both the Code of Invention and the Customization Factor to build Smartfood into the number one ready-to-eat popcorn snack, a total market estimated to be worth $134 million in 1994. He positioned his product as a premium snack for those snackers tired of chips and tacos. He customized his packaging to appeal to this audience and used extensive guerrilla marketing—actually taking the product to the street to meet snackers. His competitors at Frito-Lay finally had no choice but to buy Smartfood.

An Exercise in Custom Factoring

Illustrators are masters of customizing personas. They have a particular talent for interpreting products in the context of the target audience. Below are three different styles of illustration, along with three product profiles. See if you can guess which illustrations belong with which profile.

Illustration 1
What does this illustration seem to be saying to the target audience?

Which profile number does this illustration belong to?

Illustration 2
What does this illustration seem to be saying to the target audience?

Which profile number does this illustration belong to?

Illustration 3
What does this illustration seem to be saying to the target audience?

Which profile number does this illustration belong to?

These profile numbers do not correspond to the illustration numbers:

Profile 1
This company was undergoing major advances in technology and company structure. This illustration was part of an annual report that explained these changes to a target audience of conservative investors.

Profile 2
This illustration was for a major government initiative for senior citizens. The most important requirement of the execution was to convey a feeling of "hope" and "growth."

Profile 3
This illustration was part of a repositioning recommended by Two Dimensions for a well-known international graphic arts supply manufacturer. The new position emphasizes a new line of technology products. The target audience is graphic artists.

Persona Tip for Business

Do you know your target audience? Really know them? What age are they? Where do they live? How much do they make? What do they do for leisure? If you have not extensively researched your audience, you should make this your number one priority. You should not contemplate building a new persona for your company until you know everything there is to know about your audience. Without this knowledge, you cannot customize your persona.

Persona Tip for Entrepreneurs

You have the incredible flexibility of being your own boss. Use this flexibility, as Jeff Krief did, to find your customized niche. Don't compete with the big guns. The money often lies in the markets the big companies bypassed. Look for a Smartfood opportunity. You can choose to develop your ideas from two directions:

★   From your target audience: your ideas will flow from the audience you intend to sell to.
★   From your product or service: your product or service will become customized to suit your audience.

Find your unique niche and guerrilla-market your way to success.

Persona Tip for Salespeople

One of the biggest mistakes a salesperson can make is to write or memorize a script. Throw away any sales manual that suggests you follow a script. A script is a plan only. You must be able to customize your presentation to the specific needs and reactions of your prospect. It is critical that you not refer to a written list of "answers to objections" and other overly rigid sales techniques. Salespeople have to be very versatile to succeed. Too firm a handshake can turn away a timid prospect. A joke at the wrong time can kill a deal. Lunching with a client can lose you a customer through an inadvertent slip in manners. Salespeople must learn to customize and improvise. Without true interactivity, the customer is not participating in the sale. Without participation, there will not be closure.

Persona Tip for Employees

Every office has a professional culture. At Burger King you wear a uniform and mop with a smile. In a major law firm, you wear conservative attire and respect the established hierarchy. Whatever the culture, you must be visible. Certainly, you must respect all the rules and standards of your office. But you must differentiate yourself as superior in some way to be noticed by your employer. Usually, the manner in which you do this should be subtle and persistent. Shouting for attention in the office can be as disastrous as shouting for attention in product advertising. Inventory your personal assets. What are your key strengths? What do you do better than anyone

else? Everyone has at least one major asset. Find it, and make sure the whole office knows it. Be the apparently quiet hero who solves problems, but make sure that your boss notices. Don't shove memos of your triumph under your employer's door; instead, drop hints and evidence of your accomplishments in less obvious places. Start good rumors about yourself. Customize your persona to the needs of your employer, capitalizing on your real strengths but emphasizing the culture of the office.

Personal Persona Tip

When was the last time you tried to sell an idea to your significant other? Probably yesterday. Every day, we are selling ideas to our boss, our spouse, our friends: a trip to the cottage, a move to a bigger house, a party next Friday. Whether you are pitching your product to your prospect or a new car to your family, the principle of the Custom Factor applies equally. If you're planning a trip to Florida, your campaign will be different depending on whether you must convince your spouse or your kids. You take your knowledge of your target audience—your teenager's attitude is different from that of your twelve-year-old—and present your pitch in a way that will appeal to that audience.

The Credibility Factor

▼

Your persona must be believable and based on values with which your target audience can empathize.

Definition

Truth is an important requirement, but the credibility of your truth is more important. Your persona must in every way seem believable. Many ventures have failed because their message seemed incredible—even though it was completely true. You will have no opportunity to explain why your incredible persona is the truth. We advocate Reverse-Imaging whenever your credentials or expertise are so good no one will believe them. Reverse-Imaging is softening and weakening your incredible image, instead of boasting about your strengths. Significantly, the persona must strike a chord of direct empathy with the target audience.

What It Means

"The truth must dazzle gradually...."
Emily Dickinson

The notion of "too good to be true" has undermined many major advertising campaigns. Your truth must be credible. It doesn't matter if you can prove it. You are rarely given the opportunity to offer proof once your incredible claim is exposed to your audience.

Many of our clients at Two Dimensions: Advertising by Design have credentials that are too good. We know our clients' claims are truthful, but in most cases, we doubt that their audience will believe them. Cynicism is a normal human reaction to bold claims.

Unless you have a perfectly low-key, credible claim, in which case your offering will likely pack very little impact, you will need a carefully crafted Persona Plan. You must bring seemingly incredible facts into the range of believability for your target audience.

You have limited opportunity to capture the audience's attention and then convince them of your claim. Regardless of what media you use to promote your image, you have seconds, not minutes, to sell your claim. Unless you can confidently and conclusively prove your claim in five words or less, you have no hope of gaining credibility. It is usually impossible to gain credibility when you are making bold claims. The same is true of clever claims. Smart or overly cheeky headlines and ad styles often destroy credibility, thereby damaging Image-Equity.

Our basic formula recommendations are:
★   My offer is extremely credible and dull = use clever, witty, and exciting personas.
★   My offer is true, but my claim is hard to prove = use careful and credible personas.
★   My offer can be proven but is really incredible = let only the facts speak for you.

Don't vary far from these basic formulas. They apply to any industry. Don't let your ad agency or your marketing manager talk you into that award-winning, excruciatingly clever campaign if it will destroy your credibility. Only one type of venture can benefit from clever and exciting campaigns: those with credible messages and dull images. You can use a more exciting message if you can easily prove your claim. Otherwise, let the facts shine through with cautious persona structures.

There are many great advertising campaigns—many of them top award winners—that just don't work. This is because they are brilliant, clever, beautiful, well crafted—and totally inappropriate for the company being advertised. If your agency doesn't take considerable time to research you and your clients, it should be immediately dismissed. Both your agency and your internal marketing staff must address your audience, understand your offering, reach your audience, and captivate. This means they can't just produce high-impact advertising. They must produce credible, memorable, appropriate-impact advertising. Image is Persona Factor 1, and impact is a major component of the image mix. But Credibility is Factor 2 and equally important. Don't settle for only part of the formula.

Truth is far less important than credibility, because you have only seconds to prove your case. Your more extraordinary claims—the true claims that are harder to prove quickly—must "dazzle gradually" to help build your credibility.

Credibility Factoring Techniques

Credibility is the second-most-important element in building a persona, after image. First, you must be noticed (image), then you must be believed (credibility). Without credibility, the most clever of images is worthless. To measure your credibility, carefully calculate your Persona Credibility Index (see credibility exercise in this chapter) and follow this advice:

★ Avoid words such as best, only, first, top, lowest price guaranteed, superb, excellent, magnificent, wonderful, can't be beat, super, super low, and other such unbelievable and valueless descriptions.

★ If you can't prove your claim in fewer than five words (see the exercise in Factor 3, the Custom Factor), modify your claim so that it *can* be easily proven.

★ If you like your ads and image very much, you should doubt that your audience does. It is rare that the principals of a venture also represent the target audience. In any case, the principals always view their business through rose-colored glasses.

★ Instead of using descriptions, try using facts in your headlines and ads. Instead of "the fastest computer processor available," for example, try "a clock speed of 120mhz means you'll never watch the clock." Or, if you think the audience won't accept even this level of cleverness, try just stating cold facts, period.

★ Insist on knowing the background, research, and rationale for any marketing your consultants or agencies create and how it was tested.

The Story of Charlene Thomson

Charlene Thomson had been with MacIntyre & Gamble since graduating from college, where she made the honors list and was considered a choice draft. Nine years later, she was still working at a desk in the bullpen.

She earned her CPA degree in night school, raking in top scores. She excelled in courses in investment. At work, her analysis was always perfect and never questioned. Yet she was invisible. She saw her less experienced friends promoted to senior management. She survived a ruthless downsizing by management that eliminated 20 percent of the jobs at MacIntyre & Gamble. She tried everything to get noticed. Every time her analysis proved correct, she made sure people knew about it.

Finally, fed up, Charlene asked for an appointment with her manager. She asked him why she was always passed over for promotion. She was one of the best analysts in the firm and a certified accountant. He answered her question with a question. "Why should we consider you? What is so special about you, Char?" She stared at him in surprise. There were so many things, so much hard work, so many brilliant analyses. How could he ask such a question?

That night, she sat at her kitchen table and wrote a list of all her accomplishments. The list was several pages long and very impressive. She realized the problem was not that she didn't have the qualifications. So she started a new page, listing the accomplishments of MacIntyre & Gamble. She could think of only six. The next day in the office she scouted for other great things to say about her firm. She thought of only two more. She realized that they were no better than any other investment firm. She was at an all-time low. She found it difficult to sleep, and her appetite dropped off.

When Charlene lay awake, unable to sleep, she found herself thinking about her company instead of herself. The idea hit her in the middle of the night. She was a goal-oriented dynamo in an environment that didn't encourage dynamism. With this new perspective, she stayed up the rest of the evening making notes and thinking her idea through.

Most investment firms were "old boys clubs" catering to mostly male clientele. Most of the staff at the firm was male, and all of the promoted employees had been male.

The idea grew. Charlene would propose that she pursue an initiative to target professional women as potential new investors. She was her own target group, so she knew just how to go about it. Selling the idea to her 52-year-old male boss was no small matter, however. She decided that he would be very unreceptive to the idea. She would have to gradually place the idea in his head, reinforce it daily, and, finally, let him think it was his idea. Then she would take over the enterprise and use it to make her play for the top. She would play the old-boys game by "playing dumb but intuitive," so her conservative boss would not feel threatened.

Charlene started off by using her analytical skills to compile statistics on relevant data. How many women currently invest through MacIntyre & Gamble? How many women investors are there? How many professional women with disposable incomes are there who are not investors currently? She charted her evidence and built a substantial rationale for her idea. But she still didn't present it to her boss. She had to prepare him.

One day at the coffee machine, Charlene casually asked, "Why do you think we have so few women as customers?" Her boss didn't know. They talked about the idea for a while, and finally—"on his own"—he suggested she find out. Charlene smiled and agreed. Two days later, she surprised him with a completely researched report—a report that should have taken weeks. He hid his surprise and threw her proposal on the bottom of his "to do" pile.

Charlene couldn't bear the waiting. Two weeks passed, and she had not heard a word from her boss. Through the windows of his office she could see her report—still on the bottom of the pile.

A month and a half later, he called her to his office. "You put a lot of work into this." For a moment she thought he was going to criticize her sense of priorities. "I can see a lot of potential here, Char. Would you be interested in developing this business?"

She couldn't play the persona game any longer. She said yes so quickly that he was amused. "I can see you are very interested."

Charlene turned a sleepless night idea into more than $500,000 in new business within a few months. She had used Reverse-Imaging to make herself credible. Her new initiative was the only growth area of MacIntyre & Gamble that fiscal year. A year later, her boss got his long overdue promotion to vice president, and she got his job. Two years later, she herself became vice president.

Persona Profile: Pentium vs. PowerPC

Blue chip means credibility. When Intel launched its fastest PC processor ever, the ultimately ill-fated Pentium, it had the credibility to support its claim of the "world's fastest PC chip." But PowerPC from Motorola had actually beaten Pentium to the punch.

Is being first more valuable than being instantly credible? On the contrary, in this case, Intel swept the market with its $15 million campaign. It didn't need as long to establish credibility, because it already had a sterling reputation in the industry, so being second was not a handicap. PowerPC required weeks of expensive advertising just to establish that it was a contender. Supported by a $10 million campaign, PowerPC has achieved this status, but only as a second-place player to Pentium. It didn't matter that it was first in the market. It was not first in the credibility sweepstakes.

Does it matter who has the better product? In fact, PowerPC is less expensive and faster than Pentium. But Intel's blue-chip credibility continues to monopolize 74 percent of the world market. In the end, the credibility of its blue-chip claim was more powerful than the actual truth that PowerPC was the better product.

An Exercise in Credibility Factoring

The Persona Credibility Index (PCI) is crucial to developing an accurate Persona Plan that will guarantee success. This is why we anchor all of our Persona formulas to the Persona Credibility Index. The complete Persona Credibility Index questionnaire follows.

Most of the questions are broad and generally stated, to allow you to interpret them as they relate to your venture. The indexing process is designed to put your venture on a mathematical par with all other competitive ventures in terms of credibility. The PCI is meaningful in general terms as an indication of your credibility in the eyes of your audience.

The Persona Credibility Index

The Persona Credibility Index (PCI)[5] measures the credibility of your current positioning. All questions are answered with ratings between one and ten.

The PCI is the most important index of the formal Persona Process, because this rating is a foundation for the Persona Inventory Composite Index (PIC) and affects the score of your Persona Compromise Quotient (PCQ). These numbers are fundamental to your overall Persona Plan.

What the PCI means

PCI of 1 — An overall index of 1 is average. This indicates average credibility to the target audience or audiences. An average index indicates the need for a focused Persona Plan.

PCI below 1 — An index below 1 indicates extremely high credibility, but one that is yoked to an uninspiring and somewhat dry message that does not particularly interest the target audience. An index below 1 indicates a strong need for a dramatic and impacting persona.

PCI above 1 — An index above 1 indicates a somewhat incredible message that is not well accepted by your target audience. This requires Reverse-Imaging, or a general toning down of the persona.

Instructions

★ Answer all the questions below as accurately as you are able. If you do not know the definitive answer, ask those you work with and research the correct answer. No question should be left unanswered. Engage professional help if you cannot answer a question with 100 percent certainty.

★ Rate your answers as indicated for each question, interpreting the question to your specific venture. The PCI works for more than business planning. You can even interpret questions on different levels—such as personal pursuits, workplace goals, and so on.

★ Revise your PCI when your situation changes.

★ Read all the footnotes for clarification of the questions and instructions.

1. **Your overall positioning statement to your main target audience.**

   Write your main positioning statement in one sentence:[6]

   Describe your main target audience:[7]

   Rate the believability of your positioning statement to your target audience:[8]
   - Rate 10 for "Seems highly exaggerated even though it is completely true."
   - Rate 8 for "Seems vague and unsubstantiated."
   - Rate 6 for "Seems believable but not without some proof."
   - Rate 3 for "Seems believable with or without proof."
   - Rate 1 for "Seems to be unquestionably true."

   Rating: 1 2 3 4 5 6 7 8 9 10

   Determine your primary audience's client share:[9] _____%

   Multiply your rating in question 1 by the client share percentage figure above:[10]
   _____ x _____% = _____10

   Final Rating: _____

2. **Your secondary positioning for believability to your target audience.**

   Write your secondary positioning statement:[11]

   Describe your secondary target audience:

   Rate the believability of your positioning to your target audience:
   - Rate 7 for "Seems highly exaggerated even though it is completely true."
   - Rate 6 for "Seems vague and unsubstantiated"

- Rate 5 for "Seems believable but not without some proof."
- Rate 4 for "Seems believable with or without proof."
- Rate 3 for "Seems to be unquestionably true."

Note: In the unlikely event you have *no* secondary or tertiary markets, repeat your rating from number one.

Rating: 1 2 3 4 5 6 7 8 9 10

Determine your secondary audience's client share: _____%

Multiply your answer in question 2 by your client share percentage figure:

_____ x _____% = _____

Final Rating: _____

3. **Your tertiary positioning for believability to your target audience.**
   Write your tertiary positioning statement:

   Describe your target audience:

- Rate the believability of your positioning to your audience:
- Rate 7 for "Seems highly exaggerated even though it is completely true."
- Rate 6 for "Seems vague and unsubstantiated"
- Rate 5 for "Seems believable but not without some proof."
- Rate 5 for "Seems believable with or without proof."
- Rate 4 for "Seems to be unquestionably true."

Note: In the unlikely event you have *no* secondary or tertiary markets, repeat your rating from number one.

Rating: 1 2 3 4 5 6 7 8 9 10

Determine your tertiary audience's client share: _____%

Multiply your rating in question 3 by the client share percentage figure:

_____ x _____% = _____

Final Rating: _____

4. **Rate your remaining positions for believability to your target audience.**
   Write all other positioning statements:

   Describe your remaining target audiences:

   Rate the believability of your remaining positioning messages to your audience:
   - Rate 5 for "Seems highly exaggerated even though it is completely true."
   - Rate 5 for "Seems vague and unsubstantiated."
   - Rate 4 for "Seems believable but not without some proof."
   - Rate 4 for "Seems believable with or without proof."
   - Rate 4 for "Seems to be unquestionably true."

   Note: In the unlikely event you have *no* other markets, repeat your rating from number one.

   Rating: 1 2 3 4 5 6 7 8 9 10

   Determine your remaining client shares as a percentage: _____%[12]

   Multiply your rating in question 4 by the client share percentage figure: _____ x _____% = _____

   Final Rating: _____

5. **The credibility of your main competitor's positioning to your main target audience**[13]
   Describe your main competitor:

Rate your main competitor's credibility:
- Rate 2 for "Seems highly exaggerated even though it is completely true."
- Rate 3 for "Seems vague and unsubstantiated."
- Rate 5 for "Seems believable but not without some proof."
- Rate 7 for "Seems believable with or without proof."
- Rate 8 for "Seems to be unquestionably true."

Rating: 1 2 3 4 5 6 7 8 9 10

Divide the rating by 2 if you are the market leader:

_____ ÷ 2 = _____

Final Rating: _____

6. **The credibility of your secondary competitor's positioning to your main target audience**
Describe your secondary competitor:

Rate the credibility of its positioning to the audience:
- Rate 2 for "Seems highly exaggerated even if it is completely true."
- Rate 3 for "Seems vague and unsubstantiated."
- Rate 4 for "Seems believable but not without some proof."
- Rate 5 for "Seems believable with or without proof."
- Rate 6 for "Seems to be unquestionably true."

Rating: 1 2 3 4 5 6 7 8 9 10

Divide the rating by 1.5 if you are the market leader:

_____ ÷ 1.5 = _____

Final Rating: _____

7. **Rate your main target audience's need for your offering, based on your positioning statement.**[14]
- Rate 1 for "Our offering is absolutely essential, and we own a monopoly."

- Rate 1 for "Our offering is essential, and we are the number one offering, with only one competitor."
- Rate 2 for "Our offering is essential, and we are the number one offering with many competitors."
- Rate 3 for "Our offering is essential, and we will have a monopoly, but we are just starting up."
- Rate 4 for "Our offering is essential, and we are number two by volume among several competitors."
- Rate 5 for "Our offering is desirable, and we have a monopoly."
- Rate 5 for "Our offering is desirable, and we are the number one offering, with only one competitor."
- Rate 6 for "Our offering is desirable, and we are the number one offering with several competitors."
- Rate 7 for "Our offering is essential, but we are number three choice among competitors."
- Rate 8 for "Our offering is desirable, but we have several competitors."
- Rate 8 for "Our offering is desirable but difficult to quickly explain even though we have a monopoly."
- Rate 9 for "Our offering is desirable but difficult to quickly explain, and we have competitors."
- Rate 10 for "Our offering has no existing need to our target audience, so desire must be created."
- Rate 10 for "Our offering is complex, difficult to explain, and there is no need for it."

Rating: 1 2 3 4 5 6 7 8 9 10

Multiply your rating by your score in question 1 and divide by 5: _____ x _____ ÷5 = _____

Final Rating: _____

8. **Rate your secondary target audience's need for your offering, based on your positioning statement.**
    - Rate 3 for "Our offering is absolutely essential, and we own a monopoly."
    - Rate 3 for "Our offering is essential, and we are the number

one offering, with only one competitor."
- Rate 4 for "Our offering is essential, and we are the number one offering with many competitors."
- Rate 5 for "Our offering is essential, and we will have a monopoly, but we are just starting up."
- Rate 5 for "Our offering is essential, and we are number two by volume among several competitors."
- Rate 5 for "Our offering is desirable, and we have a monopoly."
- Rate 6 for "Our offering is desirable, and we are the number one offering with only one competitor."
- Rate 6 for "Our offering is desirable, and we are the number one offering among several competitors."
- Rate 7 for "Our offering is essential, but we are number three choice among competitors in volume."
- Rate 7 for "Our offering is desirable, but we have several competitors."
- Rate 8 for "Our offering is desirable but difficult to quickly explain, and we have a monopoly."
- Rate 8 for "Our offering is desirable but difficult to quickly explain, and we have competitors."
- Rate 8 for "Our offering has no existing need to our target audience, so desire must be created."
- Rate 9 for "Our offering is complex, difficult to explain and there is no need for it."

Rating: 1 2 3 4 5 6 7 8 9 10

Multiply your rating by your score in question 1 and divide by 10: _____ x _____ ÷ 10 = _____

Final Rating: _____

9. **How well can you prove your positioning claim to your main target audience?**
   - Rate 1 for "Our claim is accepted by our audience without question."
   - Rate 2 for "Our claim is easy to prove empirically, and the proof is easy to understand."

- Rate 3 for "Our claim is easy to prove circumstantially, and the proof is easy to understand."
- Rate 4 for "Our claim is provable empirically but difficult to understand."
- Rate 5 for "Our claim is provable circumstantially but difficult to understand."
- Rate 8 for "Our claim is difficult to conclusively prove."
- Rate 9 for "Our claim cannot be proved."
- Rate 10 for "Our claim can be proved but is not believed by our target audience."

Rating: 1 2 3 4 5 6 7 8 9 10

Divide the rating by 1.5 if you are the market leader:
_____ ÷ 1.5 = _____

Final Rating: _____

10. How well can you prove your claim to your secondary target audiences?
    - Rate 2 for "Our claim is accepted by our audience without question."
    - Rate 3 for "Our claim is easy to prove empirically, and the proof is easy to understand."
    - Rate 4 for "Our claim is easy to prove circumstantially, and the proof is easy to understand."
    - Rate 5 for "Our claim is provable empirically but difficult to understand."
    - Rate 6 for "Our claim is provable circumstantially but difficult to understand."
    - Rate 7 for "Our claim is difficult to prove conclusively."
    - Rate 8 for "Our claim cannot be proved."
    - Rate 8 for "Our claim can be proved but is not believed by our target audience."

Rating: 1 2 3 4 5 6 7 8 9 10

Divide the rating by 1.5 if you are the market leader:

_____ ÷ 1.5 =_____

Final Rating: _____

11. **How long does it take to prove your claim to your main target audience?**
    - Rate 1 for "It is generally accepted by our target audience without proof."
    - Rate 2 for "We can prove our claim in one word."
    - Rate 3 for "We can prove our claim in one sentence."
    - Rate 5 for "We can prove our claim in one paragraph."
    - Rate 6 for "We can prove our claim through testimonials."
    - Rate 7 for "We can prove our claim through a collection of proofs."
    - Rate 9 for "We can prove our claim scientifically, but it is difficult to explain."
    - Rate 10 for "Even though we can prove our claim, it is not widely believed by our target audience."

    Rating: 1 2 3 4 5 6 7 8 9 10

    Divide your rating by 1.5 if you are the market leader:

    _____ ÷ 1.5 = _____

    Multiply your net rating by 3 if your claim is UNTRUE:

    _____ x 3 = _____

    Final Rating: _____

12. **How long does it take to prove your claim to your secondary target audience?**
    - Rate 3 for "It is generally accepted by our target audience without proof."
    - Rate 5 for "We can prove our claim in one sentence."
    - Rate 6 for "We can prove our claim in one paragraph."
    - Rate 6 for "We can prove our claim through a collection of proofs."
    - Rate 6 for "We can prove our claim through testimonials only."

- Rate 7 for "We can prove our claim scientifically, but it is difficult to explain."
- Rate 8 for "Even though we can prove our claim, it is not widely believed by our target audience."

Rating: 1 2 3 4 5 6 7 8 9 10

Divide your rating by 1.5 if you are the market leader:
_____ ÷ 1.5 = _____
Multiply your rating by 2 if your claim is untrue:
_____ x 2 = _____

Final Rating: _____

13. **Rate the strength of your warranty or guarantee.**
    - Rate 1 for "We have the longest time guarantee in our market with no conditions."
    - Rate 3 for "We have the longest time guarantee in our market with conditions."
    - Rate 4 for "We have the longest time guarantee in our market with many conditions."
    - Rate 6 for "We have the industry standard guarantee in our market."
    - Rate 8 for "We stand behind our offering 100 percent, but not in writing."
    - Rate 6 for "Guarantees and warranties are not necessarily valuable in our industry."
    - Rate 5 for "Guarantees and warranties are not needed in our industry."
    - Rate 10 for "We do not offer guarantees and warranties, even though our competitors offer them."

Rating: 1 2 3 4 5 6 7 8 9 10

Final Rating: _____

14. **Rate your positioning statement and promise flexibility.**
    - Rate 1 for "We never change our promise or positioning statement."

- Rate 3 for "We rarely change our promise, and only if it is desired by our target audience."
- Rate 4 for "We only change our promise in response to our competitors."
- Rate 8 for "We change our promise every year to remain timely."
- Rate 9 for "We change our promise every time sales or performance drops."
- Rate 10 for "We change our promise frequently."

Rating: 1 2 3 4 5 6 7 8 9 10

Final Rating: _____

15. **Rate the truth of your promises and claims**.
    - Rate 1 for "Our claims and promises are totally and empirically true."
    - Rate 2 for "Our claims and promises are totally and circumstantially true."
    - Rate 3 for "Our claims and promises are true but slightly exaggerated."
    - Rate 4 for "Our claims and promises are true but exaggerated."
    - Rate 6 for "Our claims and promises are mostly true, but we don't mention the unfavorable aspects."
    - Rate 7 for "Our claims and promises are partially true."
    - Rate 7 for "We believe our claims and promises to be true, but they cannot be proven."
    - Rate 8 for "Our audience generally believes our claims are true, but they are not."
    - Rate 10 for "Our claims and promises are untrue and are not believed to be true."

Rating: 1 2 3 4 5 6 7 8 9 10

Final Rating: _____

16. **Rate your history.**[15]
    - Rate 1 for "We were first into our market niche and are still number one."
    - Rate 2 for "We were not first into our market niche but are now number one."
    - Rate 6 for "We were first, but are now number two."
    - Rate 7 for "We were second, and are still number two."
    - Rate 9 for "We were second and are now number three."
    - Rate 10 for "We were neither second nor first and are now number four or lower."

Rating: 1 2 3 4 5 6 7 8 9 10

Final Rating: _____

17. **Rate your product's need in the target audiences.**
    - Rate 1 for "We are the only product in our category and are a necessity."
    - Rate 2 for "We are the number one supplier in our category and a necessity."
    - Rate 3 for "We are the number two supplier in our category and a necessity."
    - Rate 3 for "We are the only product in our category and highly desirable."
    - Rate 4 for "We are the number one supplier in our category and highly desirable."
    - Rate 6 for "We are the only product in our category and desirable."
    - Rate 7 for "We are the number one supplier in our category and desirable."
    - Rate 8 for "We are not the number one supplier but our offering is highly desirable."
    - Rate 10 for "Our product is not desirable."

Rating: 1 2 3 4 5 6 7 8 9 10

Final Rating: _____

Calculating Your Persona Credibility Index

★ Add all the final ratings from the 17 questions:
  Cumulative Rating: _____

★ Add your rating in Question 1, 7, 9, 11 and 15:
  _____ + _____ + _____ + _____ + _____ = _____

  Result: _____

★ Add your results from step 1 and 2 (immediately above):
  _____ + _____ = _____
  Rating: _____

★ Divide your result in step 3 by 20:
  _____ ÷ 20 = _____
  Result: _____

★ Divide your result in step 4 by 5 to determine your Persona Credibility Index:
  _____ ÷ 5 = _____

PERSONA CREDIBILITY INDEX RATING:

WHAT IT MEANS:

Your rating is	Believability	Excitement	Action
.50 or lower	Extremely believable	Extremely dull	Need radical Persona Plan
.50-.60	Very credible	Dull image	Need an inspiring persona
.60-70	High credibility	Still yawning	Spice it up!
.70-80	Everyone believes you	You bore them	Dress it up!
.80-90	Conservative	Try harder	Liven it up!
1.0	**Credible and average**	**Average**	**Cautious excitement can't hurt**
1.0-1.1	Credible	Ho-hum	Be cautious in claims
1.1-1.2	Reasonably credible	You're interesting	Don't overdo it
1.2-1.3	Mostly believable	You're fun	Be slightly conservative
1.3-1.4	Somewhat believable	You're exciting	Tone down your image
1.5 and over	You must prove it	You're thrilling	Don't exaggerate—be rational

Persona Tip for Business People

The most important thing you can do in planning your marketing is to determine your credibility to your audience. The most measured method is to complete the Persona Credibility Index. Informal analysis is fine, as long as you are realistic in your appraisal. Formal market research may be necessary to determine the answers to some of the PCI questions. If you have a sizable marketing budget or audience you should consider polling with variations of these questions. Whatever type of research you do, use the values that result to complete your Persona Credibility Index.

The PCI will tell you if your audience believes your offering's claim. Study your competitors. If they seem more credible because of their marketing image, their years in the business, or their reputation, you may never be able to convince the audience that you are better. The best tip in this scenario is to determine what claim will be believed. Do some informal testing, or have your salespeople ask their prospects.

Persona Tip for Entrepreneurs

Credibility is a difficult mission for a new venture. Why should anyone believe your claims? You have not proven them in the marketplace. The start-up venture must build credibility slowly. Claims of being better than established competitors are always highly suspect in the audience's mind. Every market has a different method of proving its claims, but even irrefutable proof is limited in value to the entrepreneur who is just starting up. There are two possible approaches to this scenario:

- ★ Build an image that totally avoids the start-up issue, by appearing well established from day one.
- ★ Build your credibility gradually, never making overly confident or exaggerated claims.

As a start-up, you must treasure your credibility message above all. You must treasure every client and value every prospect's opinion. You should collect testimonials and references. Then don't wait for prospects to ask you for references; offer them yourself. You must never allow mistakes to appear in public. You must appear perfect but not be boast about it. You must be modest, sincere, and patient.

Persona Tip for Salespeople

Salespeople face many of the same issues as the start-up entrepreneur. Unless they work for a well-established blue chip company, they have to prove their cases and establish their credibility with each prospect. Often, this is the most discouraging aspect of the sales profession. You must always start at the beginning, patiently cultivating new prospects who do not want to believe you. This is why high-pressure sales techniques no longer work. In today's climate, soft selling and quiet professionalism work best in this demanding profession—regardless of product or service. A pushy salesperson loses credibility immediately. An overly friendly salesperson suffers the same loss. Only the professional, nonthreatening, sincere salesperson who attempts to solve the prospect's genuine problems with genuine solutions can succeed over the long term.

Persona Tip for Employees

Study the story of Charlene Thomson. She knew that she could not get a promotion or even respect in her company if she came up with a brilliant idea and hit her boss on the head with it. She had to cultivate her credibility through subtle and patient strategy. She knew her boss was a moderate sexist, and she was prepared to beat him at his own sad game. She knew her company would not believe that any idea from her could be a good one, so she made it appear to be her boss's idea. Then, when the idea had credibility, she took over. You must study your own workplace to determine the attitudes of the people in your company. They are your target audience in your effort to market yourself as a candidate for a promotion or raise. Soft-sell them and let them make up their own minds.

Personal Persona Tip

Sometimes even the closest family member has difficulty believing an incredible story. Truth can be stranger than fiction. If you foiled a bank robber and were nominated for a civic medal, your family might doubt you until they saw your face on the nightly news. Credibility is never easy to achieve. Your family, however, will believe you before your friends. Your friends will believe you before your acquaintances. This is because you have built up Credibility Equity (or a liability, if you are persistently dishonest) with them. You can make a family member believe the incredible if you are not prone to unbelievable claims. But you should use this equity sparingly. Too many unsupported claims can diminish your credibility.

You have the least credibility with a stranger. Conversation with a stranger at a party is usually chock-full of "that's interesting" and "is that so?" phrases. This is true usually because the stranger grants you no credibility without proof. In all your personal ventures, keep your credibility in mind. Human beings have a natural desire to convince and sway others to their point of view. To do this successfully, you need to be credible.

The No-Compromise Factor

▼

Your Persona Plan, once established, must be treated as a set of rules that may never be broken.

Definition

Any intentional or unintentional variance from the Persona Plan weakens equity in the persona. It is particularly important to be rigid in controlling the Persona Plan in the first two years, when Image-Equity is delicate. An established venture can squander Image-Equity from time to time, but start-up businesses cannot afford compromises. Control your image, your staff, and your product with religious fervor.

What It Means

"The secret of success is constancy to purpose."
Benjamin Disraeli

Larger corporations with formal corporate standards often make it a firing offense to break their image guidelines. This is a good policy for business (though less pleasant for employees). It reinforces the importance of the No-Compromise Factor. Nothing is more crucial to business than the image presented to the public. The public accepts the truth it sees, not the truth that exists. You must always make sure that what the public sees is the truth of your persona. As staff and resources grow, it becomes even more important to make the rules more rigid.

Developing a corporate culture helps maintain the formula of Persona. Kentucky Fried Chicken, Apple, and AT&T all have their own unique cultures. Even new employees are expected to quickly assimilate the cultural rules and taboos. Staff members of long standing should quickly correct breakdowns in the corporate culture.

Start-up ventures can develop a corporate culture quickly by following a rigid Persona Plan covering all aspects of visibility: staff conduct, product quality, service promise, name, logo, advertising, atmosphere in the office, and so on. The culture should be enforced with evangelical zeal—an infectious zeal that motivates customers and employees.

The entrepreneurs and managers of a firm should follow the culture more rigidly than the employees. If the corporate culture involves wearing a suit and being tidily groomed, make sure the leaders are correctly suited and groomed each and every day.

This approach should not be interpreted as mindlessly rigid. If your culture is artistic and you believe your clients expect casual appearance, formal dress becomes the taboo of the company: no suits allowed. If you are running a plumbing operation, trade dress may be part of the culture, or you may wish to stand apart by being the only plumbers in town who dress in designer clothing. Set the culture—and never vary from it.

No-Compromise Factoring Techniques

The most important thing you can do to ensure no-compromise is to have a written plan—a step-by-step plan with dates, deadlines, guidelines, rules, and consequences for failing in any of these areas:

★ Being consistent. This is as important as not compromising. Short-term no-compromises are valueless. You must never compromise.

★ Laying down the rules and culture of a venture or division of a venture from the very beginning.

- ★ Setting a no-compromise example. For example, if you have a rule that says no one can take a holiday in the busy season, you must follow it yourself.
- ★ Writing memos, contracts, and messages and asking those involved to read and sign them.

The Story of Jenny Gray

Jenny Gray was not what you might call a "tough boss." She liked people and people liked her. Discipline was never her forte. She had never needed to be tough as the one-person marketing department at Michele Cosmetics.

In 1987, Michele Cosmetics' fiercest rival, Body Beautiful, hired her away. It was a bigger company, and she was offered a senior position as Marketing Director over a team of eleven people. Her salary dramatically increased—and so did her stress.

At first, after she overcame her feelings of guilt and betrayal, Jenny found Body Beautiful exciting. It was a busy head office with a vibrant energy that was still humming late into the night. She wasn't sure she'd make the perfect boss, but she was determined not to make any mistakes. She made her first one within weeks, when she invited her team out for a get-acquainted lunch. In the first three months, she became close to her team and even began socializing with them.

It had been easy at Michele Cosmetics. Jenny had made decisions, then acted on those decisions. Body Beautiful was far more complex. She made a decision, someone organized a meeting, they discussed it, changed it, qualified it, rationalized it, then assembled a team to execute it. By the time her brilliant concepts were executed, they were not even remotely similar to her original idea. She tried talking to her staff—her friends—explaining how she wanted her ideas to be implemented as she had originally instructed. They told her that the committee approach was the way Body Beautiful had always worked.

The results were not spectacular. The ad agency—hired by a committee—created a campaign that was anything but a campaign. Sales were not dropping yet, but Jenny knew she had to act quickly.

It went against her nature, but Jenny sat down behind her closed door and wrote up a long list of rules for her staff. She wrote a complete Marketing Plan and asked each of the staff to read and follow it. Then she began the series of tough lectures that left her weak-kneed and teary-eyed. She was becoming the tough boss.

Three weeks later she fired the ad agency. Two of her staff members resigned. She let another go. They didn't have lunch with her anymore. But things started to change. They started to do things her way. Her ideas were rarely changed, and they were all consistent with the Marketing Plan she had developed. The new agency developed a brilliant strategic campaign that launched a consistent persona for Body Beautiful.

Jenny's only regret was that she had lost her friends. She realized that she had started their relationship incorrectly, that had she exerted control from the beginning, her staff might like her better. But her staff did respect her. When market share increased, Jenny moved up and now she is vice president at Body Beautiful.

Persona Profile: Ford Under Caldwell

His war cry was "Quality Is Job Number One." Philip Caldwell, the first nonfamily member to run the Ford Motor Company., was out to change the culture. Once it was changed, he would allow no compromise.

Ford automobiles had become poor-quality boxes that both looked and drove dated. Japanese cars were flooding the market. All of the U.S. auto makers were struggling, their market shares dwindling. Ford was also struggling with the expensive burden of federal safety and fuel mileage standards. It was a grim time for Ford.

Caldwell developed a new plan, which changed the persona and fate of Ford Motor Company forever. He issued the mandate that "Quality Is Job Number One," and to back it up, he rebuilt the entire company. Factories were restructured, the entire car line redesigned, and every job description was covered in the review. The new line was to consist of efficient, attractive, and quality automobiles.

The Taurus was the first major turnaround car for the fortunes of Ford. They had done everything right. The car was sleek, attractive, fuel efficient, and well assembled. The promise of "quality" had been delivered. Ford's credibility began to return, and its market share grew from 16 percent to 19 percent, with Taurus becoming the best-selling car in America.

Caldwell had ruthlessly turned the company around. He compromised on none of his ideals. He had carefully planned his success. The quality image became the company's war cry and its persona.

An Exercise in No-Compromise Factoring

This exercise reproduces the process of determining the Persona Compromise Quotient. The Persona Compromise Quotient is an important second step in the Persona Planning technique. You will need this quotient value to complete your Persona Inventory (see Part 5, A Persona How-To).

Persona Compromise Quotient[16]

The Persona Compromise Quotient (PCQ) measures your willingness to compromise objectives and standards to achieve short-term needs.[17] Compromise is damaging to any persona.

What the PCQ means

PCQ of 10—This is average. Strive for improvement by adding consequences to your rules. Set a strong example.

PCQ below 10—This an indication that you or your venture are uncompromising. There's nothing wrong with this, provided your rigidity impacts staff morale or client opinions.

PCQ above 10—This is a significant warning to become more rigid in implementing your standards, plans, and goals. Failure to do so makes all Persona Planning a futile exercise.

Instructions

★ Fill in your Persona Credibility Index Number (PCI).[18]
   PCI Total Value: ____
★ Answer all the questions below as accurately as you are able.
★ Rate your answers as indicated in each question, interpreting the question to your specific venture.
★ Revise your PCQ when your situation changes.
★ Read all the footnotes for clarification of the questions and instructions.

1. **Rate your venture's ability to compromise.**
   • Rate 5 if "We are not able to compromise because of our rigid structure."
   • Rate 4 if "Our structure makes compromise difficult, but we never do because we follow our plans."
   • Rate 3 if "We are able to compromise, but we rarely do, because we know how important plans are."
   • Rate 2 if "We are able to compromise and often do because our short-term goals are important."
   • Rate 1 if "We are constantly compromising, because we have no plan or we are just getting started."

   Rating: 1 2 3 4 5   **Total Rating:** _____

2. **When do you compromise your plans?**
   - Rate 5 if "We never compromise."
   - Rate 4 if "We compromise only when we have no choice."
   - Rate 3 if "We compromise only in an emergency."
   - Rate 2 if "We compromise only on minor or internal matters."
   - Rate 1 if "We are constantly compromising."

   Rating: 1 2 3 4 5   **Total Rating:** _____

3. **Rate your visual standards enforcement.**
   - Rate 5 if "A violation of our visual standards results in dismissal."
   - Rate 4 if "A violation of our visual standards results in stern warnings and eventual dismissal."
   - Rate 3 if "Our standards are loosely enforced."
   - Rate 2 if "We have standards but rarely enforce them."
   - Rate 1 if "We never enforce our standards or do not have any."

   Rating: 1 2 3 4 5   **Total Rating:** _____

4. **Rate which of the following would force you to compromise.**
   - Rate 5 if "We never compromise."
   - Rate 4 if "Competitive pressure."
   - Rate 4 if "Client pressure."
   - Rate 3 if "Time pressure."
   - Rate 2 if "Staff pressure."
   - Rate 1 if "Peer pressure."

   Rating: 1 2 3 4 5

If you would be likely to compromise for more than one of these reasons, subtract one for any additional pressures you would succumb to:[19] _____ - _____ = _____

N.B. If your value is negative, be sure to enter as a negative in brackets and subtract from your cumulative total.

Total Rating: _____

Calculate your cumulative total
Total Rating Score: _____

Divide your total rating score by your Persona Credibility Index Rating:[20]

_____ ÷ _____ = _____

Your Persona Compromise Quotient Is _____

What It Means

1. A rating below 5 is a disaster. You need urgent action *before* commencing with your Persona Plan. Your Plan will be worthless until you correct your ridiculous tendency to compromise.
2. A rating of 5–8 needs some work. You can get by, but your tendency to compromise is going to weaken the effectiveness of your Persona Plan. No matter how good your Plan is, compromise will dilute your chances for success. Take immediate action to improve the situation.
3. A rating of 8–12 is in the average zone. You are probably okay; 10 is average. Don't be too pleased, however, if you are average. Try to reduce your tendency to innovate or make decisions on the fly. You may get lucky, but you weaken your long-term position. Be vigilant and improve.
4. A rating of 12–16 is very good from an image-building point of view. Be cautious, though, that you do not appear too rigid.
5. A rating over 16 is probably too high. You should maintain your valuable tendency not to compromise, but soften your rigid rules just enough so that everyone is comfortable and you have flexibility to deal with urgent situations.

Persona Tip for Business People

The most important first step in preventing compromises is to have written guidelines for anything that is visible to your prospective clients. You should have office standards, encompassing cleanliness, personal items, and decor, which are all based on your persona. If you have a separate marketing department, it should follow strict company guidelines—especially relating to company positioning and corporate visual identities. Staff must be instructed how to write letters and use promotional support materials.

But having written guidelines is only a first step. Without enforcement, they are soon forgotten—in most cases, stuffed in the back of a filing cabinet, never to be referred to again. There must be clear and known consequences for violations. You have to make it clear to all staff that the purpose and consequences of the rules is not to lower staff morale, but to impress clientele. Image should come first. Consistency is a close second. Never allow exceptions to the rules. If you compromise your own rules by not enforcing them, how can you prevent compromises to your larger plans for success?

Persona Tip for Entrepreneurs

Develop a Marketing Plan, a Persona Plan, and a precise Business Plan. Nothing is more important to the entrepreneur than planning. Don't venture into business without these three plans. Even if you are well funded, very lucky, and have angels at your back, you cannot succeed without real planning. Real planning means setting meaningful and realistic goals and developing methods of achieving them. Unrealistic goals will rapidly defeat you—frustrating all your efforts and making your angels fly back to their clouds forever. Going into business without a plan is analogous to going to war without a general or a strategy. The best you can hope for without a plan is survival by the seat of your pants. If you have a realistic plan—a realistic plan that you follow diligently—you should be victorious.

Persona Tip for Salespeople

Salespeople are often more prone to compromise than their companies. It's a common stereotype: the salesperson taking the side of a client to convince his manager to compromise the pricing or other company standards.

The salesperson loses respect and credibility every time he agrees to "go to bat for the customer." The customer knows you are not on his side. You are the company's representative. The client knows you are insincere. Try a new method. A firm stance—gently presented with sensitivity to the prospect's responses—can gain you respect. Unless you have done a poor job of qualifying and handling objections, your posture should make your product seem more desirable. A willingness to compromise price is usually a sign of a poor product or above-value pricing. The salesperson who chases a prospect out the door will never close a deal. A willingness to let someone walk is an important tactic in sales. If you haven't the strength to stand by your company's principles, either you don't belong in sales or you don't belong with your company.

Persona Tip for Employees

Perfection in the workplace may be an impossibility, but appearing perfect is not. As valuable as friendships are—and many of us socialize more at work than at home—it is difficult to prevent damaging compromises with companions. We gossip more, empathize more, fraternize more, defend more, joke more, and are generally more comfortable with our friends. But often the jokes, emotions, and friendships get in the way of promotion. To appear perfect—to prevent exposing your weaknesses—you must avoid close friendships in the workplace. This does not mean that you should not have friends. The nature of friendships forged in the workplace is warm but controlled. You have to be careful about gossiping; it has a way of getting back to your boss. You have to avoid tasteless jokes. You have to stay cool, even when the boss trashes your friends. Otherwise you and your friends will stay where you are without hope of advancement. Don't turn your back on your friends or become a robot. Just impose some no-compromise standards on everything you say and do at work, and you will find the barriers dropping and the boss paying attention.

Personal Persona Tip

You never know whom you might run across in public. You might meet your top client at the mall. The slow driver you cut off on the freeway might be the prospect you've been trying to land. You might gossip about someone without realizing he's standing behind you at the party. The same no-compromise standards from business apply in your personal life, to the degree you wish to profit from them. Grooming and dressing neatly on your "personal time" may seem uncomfortable, but personal reputations are not irrelevant to your associates and clients. Be aware that all you say and do in your personal life, even if it is your own business, may be visible to those who could be offended by it. Treat others with respect, and always put your best foot forward.

The Growth Factor

▼

If you follow your Persona Plan carefully, your endeavor will grow at a compound rate until, at maturity, Persona Equity grows on its own.

Definition

Investing in your image will pay dividends eventually in terms of equity value. You should never make a Persona withdrawal before the Persona bank account reaches the self-growing level. Compromise, or failure to implement a step in the Persona Plan, will damage equity severely and set back the value of the image severalfold. Steadfastly maintaining your Persona Plan with evangelical zeal will build such value in your image that soon you won't need to spend time building your persona. Your audience will just know you are what you claim. Your reputation will grow with mathematical certainty, like compound interest on your bank account.Then, carefully, you can begin to spend your hard-earned success.

What It Means

"Growth itself contains the germ of happiness."
Pearl S. Buck

To the Young

Growth comes only to those with patience. Beings with the higher intelligences, such as humans, take the longest to develop to maturity. But that long road leads to the most spectacular of intellects, which includes imagination, inspiration, memory, and growth. The persona must also grow slowly. The persona will experience growth and change and mistakes just like a growing person. The persona must learn and evolve. Your image must be treated almost as a separate entity. Once the persona is learned—as the child learns about life through adventures and mistakes—it becomes powerful. The mature persona has value and worth. Clients will expect your venture to fulfill the promise of the persona. You will no longer have to prove your claims. You will have rock-hard credibility.

When you get to this fortunate position, you can profit greatly from your persona. You can trade on the strength of your reputation—

charging more for your service, creating a family of brands, opening branch offices, trading internationally, and reducing advertising costs, because your reputation makes it unnecessary. These are the benefits of a growth persona.

Even though the first five Persona Factors can give you credibility, visibility, and success, long-term value comes from consistency and growth. You should never stop supporting your persona. As you grow, your image should be sacred. Any ad agency or employee who damages image should be disciplined. Likewise, any ad agency or employee who grows Image-Equity should be rewarded. Nothing is more profitable in the long term than being able to trade on your hard-earned fame. Some great personas even sell their names once they build them up. Franchises are formed around solid persona bases. The more famous the persona, the more expensive the license. Movie stars sell their names for endorsements, charging millions. Their name is their image. But give that movie star a single scandal, and the name is not worth one penny. O. J. Simpson and Michael Jackson are no longer valuable commodities. Their images have been severely damaged.

Protect and grow your persona. It is your most valuable possession.

Growth Factoring Techniques
Growth comes from nurturing. Consistency of application of your persona is the steady road to success. Little mistakes damage. Big mistakes destroy. Try to:

★   Follow the previous five Persona Factors carefully and consistently.
★   Treat your venture or company as a separate entity—no matter how small or principal-driven the structure. Even a sole proprietor should name and nurture his persona as a completely separate entity.
★   Do not allow any variances from your rigid Persona Plan until your venture is well established. This step is only achieved when virtually your entire target audience thinks of your venture first.
★   Once you've achieved this stature, trade on the value of your persona to profit through expansion, co-branding, and price increases.

The Story of Gordon Roberts

Roberts Milk grew from a delivery milk service in the fifties to become one of Metro's largest dairies. It diversified into many products, selling under various brand names. It sold yogurt, milk, eggs, eggnog, ice cream, lactose-free milk products, and soy milk.

Although profitable in the fifties, Gordon Roberts's business could not be maintained in the nineties. The well-known company had not turned a profit in a decade. Gordon attributed the company's performance to the recession and the rising unpopularity of milk resulting from poor press about the use of growth steroids in cows.

To counteract the company's direction, Gordon increased his substantial advertising budget, added new lines of products to trade on his valuable name, and lowered his prices. Still revenues and profits dropped. He began an unplanned run of layoffs to try to return his company to profitability. Finally, though never a believer in the value of consultants, Gordon became desperate enough to hire a marketing consultant.

The marketing consultant studied every aspect of Gordon's dairy: staff, offices, quality, clientele, price, packaging, advertising, product lines, positioning. Gordon couldn't believe the advice or the fees, but he listened. He listened because he had tried virtually everything else.

The marketing consultant told him to go back to his core business. He had been famous in the fifties for delivering bottled milk straight to people's doorsteps. Nothing else. Everybody in the area used to drink Roberts Milk. Following the consultant's strange advice, Gordon withdrew from the yogurt, soy milk, ice cream, egg, and eggnog markets. He focused on milk. He even brought back fresh-milk-to-the-door service in some neighborhoods. He date-stamped his milk products more prominently and changed the shape of his bottles to resemble his fifties-style packaging. His advertising trumpeted a wholesome theme—no steroids, only the freshest milk—and reminded nostalgic customers of Roberts bottled milk.

▲ Code of Continuity

Two Dimensions produced this inexpensive Image-Marketing flyer to keep the agency in the audience's mind. It supports the agency's fun culture with striking imagery, wacky themes, and diverse creative styles. Whatever your image, follow your Persona Plan without compromise.

▲ Spotting Success

SPOTS, an expensive, carefully crafted Image-Marketing brochure, gave Two Dimensions instant visibility and credibility, essential to any venture. It has won numerous international awards and generated $300,000 in revenue within months.

▲ Spotting the Differences

"The Thinker" pointedly emphasizes the Unique Selling Point of Two Dimensions—that 2D is Canada's strategic-creative agency. Whether you are creating a company or a brochure, apply as many of the Persona Factors and Codes as you can. Carefully plan your success.

▲ A Spotlight on Credibility

Here SPOTS highlights testimonials, powerful credibility statements when they come from credible sources. With its oversized extravagance, SPOTS uses the Image Factor to "demand" attention.

▲ The Spotty Mascots

SPOTS grew out of our logo (see A Two Dimensional Model) and featured our living logos, DJ and Portia. Our strategy was to develop the recognizable culture of a leading-edge, funky, fun ad agency. Refer to the Growth Factor and the Independence Factor.

▶ Blue Chip Image

For the launch of its important new AS/400 software, IBM asked Two Dimensions to create a product persona to appeal to sophisticated programmers. The Code of Impact was used to capture attention in a crowded, competitive market.

▼ Code of Reach

IBM's AS/400 Productivity Tools were launched with a strategic direct-mail kit sent straight to the target audience. From the unique attention-grabbing mailer box (Code of the Package) to the complete information contained within (Code of Quality), this kit was instantly credible, dramatically visible.

AS/400
PROGRAMMER
PRODUCTIVITY
TOOLS
IBM

Programming Languages

Application Dictionary Services

CODE/400

Application Development Manager

ACCURACY ▶ CONTROL ▶ EFFICIENCY ▶

AIM FOR PRODUCTIVITY

IBM

BECAUSE YOU NEED...

▲ Twin Personas

The Gemini Awards—the Canadian equivalent of the Emmy—got a new persona from Two Dimensions. The illustrated program incorporated every major printing, binding, and graphic technique possible to enhance the "star" culture and image of the event.

▲ Another Look for the Twins

The No-Compromise Factor must be taken in the context of a venture's objectives. Since the Gemini presentation is meant to honor excellence and entertain, radical image changes from year to year are a necessary strategy for maximum impact.

▲ The Movie Genie

The Genie Awards honor the persona of the movie star. For its fifteenth anniversary, we illustrated the Genie in fifteen different styles with various personas. Each illustration emulates the persona-like style of a master artist: Picasso, Monet, and others.

▲ The Academy Persona

The Academy of Canadian Cinema and Television's most important persona statement is usually its annual report. The "image of prestige" is portrayed on the report's cover by gold-oil inks. The annual report is a tremendously important element of any Persona Plan.

▲ A New Strategy For Letraset

Letraset, world famous for traditional art supplies, hired Two Dimensions to change the "collective consciousness" of its target audience. The new look for Letraset's product catalogue was the first step in a plan that repositioned the company as a purveyor of leading-edge graphic software products.

▲ It's All In the Packaging

The Code of the Package was used to change an entrenched position. We designed a hinged box that resembles software packaging with the catalogue contained inside, repositioning the product line. The striking graphics won many international awards.

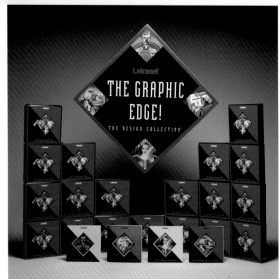

▲ What's in the Packaging

The Reality Factor demands substance. These four catalogues were contained in the "software box" along with demonstration products, a font poster, and other useful products. We called it The Design Collection and gave it a desirable persona through striking graphics.

◀ Code of the Race

The launch of The Design Collection was a tightly guarded secret for months preceding the launch. Suddenly, POP dramatically appeared in stores (featured here). This was part of a "Code of the Race" strategy: dozens of media, PR opportunities, and promotional offers were used to "race" into the audience mind.

◀ Code of the Unexpected

The unusual new catalogue from Letraset was supported by a "mystery door" teaser campaign that played on the power of the Code of the Unexpected. After launch, the mystery door campaign was supported by a "door prize" coupon promotion.

▲ Code of Advertising

Advertising is anything your audience sees or hears, from the way you answer your phone to major network TV ads. Here, CCNS reaches its highly focused target audience through trade shows. Whatever media you choose, it must project your chosen persona and employ all the codes and factors. Note the credibility tactic of using a testimonial from The Financial Post.

▶ Code of Ownership

The Code of Ownership insists that you find your niche and own it. Although many competitors offer similar services, only CCNS can offer access to all public information in Canada. This led to their most important persona statement: "There's more than one reason to rely on CCNS . . . but having all registries in one Information Place could be the only one that matters."

CCNS

▲ The Expert Persona

To portray the expert you must be the acknowledged expert. CCNS is the largest public information source in Canada but needed a new persona to grow its already dominant position. We kept the equity of the name CCNS, but permanently added the designation "The Information Place" in a new logo. The new positioning made it clear that CCNS is the source for public information.

▼ Code of Dreams

CCNS used the dreams of its clients and its own creativity to create proprietary new software. Now, for the first time, its clients can have one short summary of information instead of many pages of raw data. We sold this idea in the ads and brochures by appealing to the audience's needs: "For Those Of You Who Believe Paper Work Is Not One of Life's Priorities . . ."

▲ The Credibility Factor

Ontario tourism is worth billions of dollars annually. Research indicated that tourists want facts, not hype. Our strategy for tourism was to reinforce the "credibility" of Ontario as an exciting travel destination through unique "Trip Planners" that contained useful facts, highlights of destinations, and planning aids.

◄ A Half Million Lakes and Targeting

If you have it, make sure everyone knows it. Only Ontario offers over half a million of the most unpolluted lakes in the world. The Code of Targeting demands you address your most impressive and differentiated features to the audience who can benefit from them.

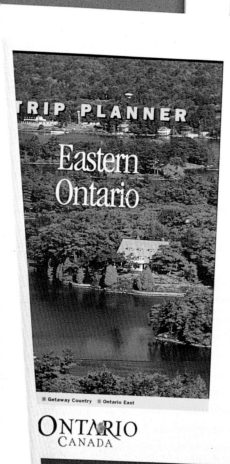

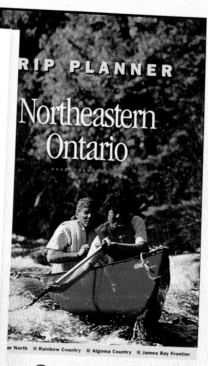

► Code of Collective Conscious

Rather than fight people's image of Ontario as a land of ice and snow, we used this perception to differentiate Ontario. Winter becomes a selling point. It is usually not worth the expense to try and change the collective conscious—no matter how wrong it might be.

▲ Code of Invention

A shopping mall is a shopping mall, right? Research indicated that shoppers believe all shopping malls to be similar. We used the Code of Invention to "break away from the pack" (Code of First Mind) by creating a new positioning statement for one of Canada's biggest shopping centers, Fairview Mall. The "Only At Fairview," promise, here shown on large in-mall signs, forces us always to invent completely original campaigns.

▲ The Age of Substance and Responsibility

The Age of Substance and Responsibility requires visible and honest efforts to be a good citizen. Fairview Mall is entirely dedicated to "giving back to the community" it serves. Here, a humorous Christmas campaign appeals to the audience's need to both give and receive (Code of Humanity). The campaign raised money for the needy while offering valuable prizes to shoppers just for "Showing Your Button."

豬年旺相

HAPPY
CHINESE
NEW
YEAR

ONLY AT FAIRVIEW

▲ Code of Targeting

Persona requires a strong focus on the audience. This campaign, targeted specifically at the Cantonese Chinese community, combines the dynamic energy of color with the sophisticated imagery of famous designer Kam Wai Yu. It has won many advertising awards, including several golds, statues, and grand prizes.

▶ No-Compromise

As always, every communication—large or small—must be consistent with the "owned" positioning. In this case, "Only at Fairview" is actually the name of a low-cost two-color newsletter.

▶ Simpatico Persona

Lonix appeals directly to its target audience by showing typical customers enjoying a favorite activity. We tagged this image with the central positioning statement "Hats That Go Anywhere You Go." An important Simpatico technique is to incorporate the word "you" in any headline.

▼ The Reality Factor

Demonstrating your truths is fundamental to your credibility. At the time we created this catalogue, Lonix was aggressively launching against an entrenched "safari-style" hat. We demonstrated its "unique difference" by showing its waterproof characteristics. This tactic was largely responsible for Lonix's penetration into over 200 retail stores.

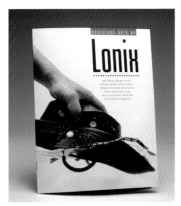

◀ Prove It!

Your audience will never believe your claims unless you can completely and quickly prove them. Lonix claims one of the world's most durable hats and proves it with detail photos and captions that explain why their hats last a lifetime.

At first revenues tumbled. Gordon had to lay off more staff. But after four months of aggressive advertising, featuring a black-and-white image of a Roberts Milk truck delivering fresh milk right to the doorstep, sales began to climb. Profits also turned, and Gordon abandoned unprofitable brands. The marketing consultant developed a simple slogan that spoke of the brand's reliability since the fifties. The company returned to its original fifties logo. Gordon himself appeared on commercials, talking about quality, freshness, and reliability.

Gordon's dairies now sell only milk. No side products. Today his name is so valuable that he could sell yogurt, lactose-free milk, and other dairy products if he wanted to. But Gordon is sticking to the formula that worked in the fifties and is still working today. His promise is consistent, his image is rigid and his products seem nostalgic, but Roberts Milk is the best known in the region. When Gordon finally does begin to diversify into co-brands, he will have the strength to win this time. In the meantime, he is content to be the king of milk.

Persona Profile: A Carnival of Growth

It all started in 1972 with a converted freighter. Today, Carnival Cruise Lines is a cruise-ship leader with $1.81 billion in sales.

Carnival must go against major cruise competitors and land-based alternatives in the crowded resort market. With a profit margin of 21 percent and tens of thousands of berths to fill, Carnival consistently leads through rigid adherence to its persona. Carnival discovered

this unique persona in the seventies, when it began advertising its cruises as "fun ships." It was the first to focus its marketing on the younger niche. It sailed right past its competitors to become one of the largest cruise lines.

The secret of Carnival's success is consistency. With the exception of failed forays into Spanish-only cruises and land resorts, both of which were quickly abandoned, Carnival has been true to its fun and youthful persona. In 1994, it saw its net incomes go up another 20 percent. Analysts see a very large potential for growth for Carnival, expecting increased fares to have little impact on the growth rate of its clientele.

An Exercise in Growth Factoring

The Growth Rating Quiz rates your potential to grow through an analysis of your current marketing efforts. You can answer the questions from the point of view of an existing business, a start-up venture or a personal plan. The Growth Rating Quiz consists of eight true or false questions. It offers insights into your methods and whether you are currently set up to take advantage of growth opportunities. Answer honestly, or don't bother with the exercise.

★ We are currently the market-share leader in our marketplace.[21]
  True   False

★ Our main claim is entirely true and provable in five words or less.
  True   False

★ We have a specific lifetime goal for the venture.[22]
  True   False

★ Our main claim is very believable and either needs no proof to be accepted by our audience or is easily proven.[23]
  True   False

★ We have written guidelines and rules that establish our image, and we follow them.[24]
  True   False

★ Our venture has grown every year since it was established.[25]
  True   False

★ We research everything we do, from staff hiring to advertising.[26]
  True   False

★ The name and identity of our corporation is well recognized and still growing.
  True   False

What It Means

★ If you can honestly claim eight Trues you have very little immediate need for any formal Persona Planning (although the 88 Persona Codes will be beneficial to any venture). Please note that this is a very simplistic True or False quiz and you should probably undertake a yearly Persona Plan even if you claim eight Trues.

★ If you can honestly claim six Trues, you are in good shape, but you must correct the two negatives. The surest route to correction is to follow the scientific steps of Persona Planning.

★ Claiming fewer than six Trues means you are not in a position to earn equity from your image and should immediately undertake a Persona Inventory and Persona Plan.

Persona Tip for Business People

Consistency is the power word for growth. Don't give up on your plans if they don't return immediate results. Many great ad campaigns and solid business plans have been abandoned too soon, before their impact could be felt. If you start to feel your plan isn't working, study it, see if you made any mistakes, review your research, and analyze your assumptions. If you made no mistakes, study your competition. Your plan has to take into account competitive plans. (After all, your rivals no doubt have a marketing plan—and they too may have read this book!) Recognize economic factors. If you have made any mistakes or your situation has changed through competitive actions or economic changes, modify your plan cautiously. We advocate a new Persona Inventory and a new Persona Plan every time your business undergoes a major change.

Don't make the mistake of abandoning a plan just because you can't find a problem. If you can't find one, it probably doesn't exist. In all likelihood, you are just expecting results too fast. Remember, the Growth Factor states that your venture will grow, but it is a geometric progression. Growth accelerates, doubling year after year. Remember that some industries take longer to grow than others. But growth will happen if you plan carefully, consistently adhere to your Plan, and wait patiently.

Persona Tip for Entrepreneurs

The waiting is hardest for a start-up situation. Often limited cash reserves, impatient venture capitalists, and your own drive for success can cause you to compromise a sound Persona Plan. You can overcome this danger by building short-term Persona Plans with easy-to-achieve goals. These shorter-term goals should still lead to your long-term goal, and the relative ease of achieving them will encourage and motivate you, your partners, and your staff.

Persona Tip for Salespeople

Salespeople, especially those on commission, will find the wait excruciating. They will feel they are doing something wrong when their consistent techniques fail to close. Some salespeople will compromise on every pitch—give anything to close the deal. This scenario is analogous to a retailer's gaining short-term business through price-slashing or promotions. The final effect is a net loss to both business and salesperson. And these compromises are irreversible. If a customer is consistently given what he wants, the next time he'll want even more. If you follow this path, you'll soon you lose your margins, your respect, and maybe even your job.

Be brave enough to walk away from a deal. Your customers will remember you next time, because you stood up for your principles (provided you didn't burn the bridge as you walked away). Sometimes they are just testing you and will come back in a day or two. Sometimes they go to your competition. You must apply a consistent standard to all your prospects. Treat them all with the same respect. Use the same Persona values: Image, Credibility, No-Comprise. You will succeed slowly, but you will grow.

Persona Tip for Employees

In the workplace, it is vital that you be consistent in your image if you are to grow in reputation. Workplaces are intimate situations—even if there are thousands in your building. You can't hide your inconsistencies. Business people, entrepreneurs, and salespeople can sometimes hide their mistakes, but it is rare that an employee can. So you must make extra effort to be consistent in your work persona. You may not be noticed immediately, but you will be noticed eventually—the way you want to be noticed. If you keep changing your persona until someone notices, they'll just think you are strange, or worse yet, flaky. Be consistent, and you will most certainly experience growth. At the very least, your employers will know you are stable and reliable.

Personal Persona Tip

Every situation benefits from consistency. Your family, friends, and associates will trust you implicitly if you have a perfect track record in trustworthiness. People will lend you money if they know you'll repay. Try to maintain a regular persona. Don't be afraid of being branded "boring" or "conservative" (in fact, your image can be quite bizarre as long as you are consistent). In the end, people will know they can rely on you. Your potential relationships with strangers will benefit from the references of your friends. Your new employer may also want personal references to find out how reliable you are. Only consistent, long-term application of your established persona will guarantee you a trust bond with those who matter to you.

The Research
Factor

▼

*The secret to total success
is knowledge.*

....

Definition

No Persona Plan can be developed until complete research has
been undertaken and understood. Before a plan can be created,
you must know what your specific objectives are, who your target
audience is, and what your unique selling proposition is.

....

What It Means

*"Knowledge is the true organ
of sight, not the eyes."*
Panchatantra

Translated by Franklin Edgerton

Research everything there is to know about your target audience, your competitors, your employees, your regional economy, and your own venture. With total knowledge on your side, you will see opportunities that others don't.

Refer back to the stories of Susan Pauling and Charlene Thomson. One aspect of their stories that is similar is that they both found opportunities through research. Susan closed her PR firm and became a sponsor-broker for the arts. Charlene discovered that her conservative firm was not taking advantage of an entire market segment. Both learned these things from an audit of their problem.

Marketing is a problem-solving exercise. You have products you need to move to the market. You must decide who your audience is, how to approach them, and how to handle the threat of competition. Only research can give you the solutions to your problems.

The foundation of the Persona Principle is knowledge. Your Persona Inventory requires extensive research: interviews with partners, bankers, clients, accountants, competitors, prospects, and so on; market research into your situation, your prospect's situation, the economic situation and so on; product research that determines your features and ultimately your benefits to the target audience; and both quantitative and qualitative research and analysis.

Don't be intimidated by the amount of research you must do. Francis Bacon once said "Knowledge is power." To have power in your industry you must have the knowledge. Certainly, all of the knowledge you will need is readily available. As Samuel Johnson said: "Knowledge is of two kinds: we know a subject ourselves, or we know where we can find information upon it."

You will already know much about your venture or proposed venture. You will be able to find out much more from your associates, partners, employees (especially salespeople), trade journals and associations, libraries, chambers of commerce, municipalities, and city departments. This information is free and may very well be sufficient. The more information you uncover, the more precise and calculated your results will be. For this reason, if you cannot find what you need to know from no-cost resources, you should consider engaging a market research company to pursue your research. Your future depends on it.

Research Factoring Techniques

Research seems to intimidate many of our students. There is no reason for this. Most of the information you'll need is already published and available at your local public library. Following are some other sources of information you might consult:

★ Federal government census information is usually a little dated but important for more global statistics.

★ Municipal governments can usually provide more up-to-date regional information.

★ Trade associations for your industry routinely conduct and pay for their own selective research, which may greatly benefit you.

★ Published almanacs are broad-stroked but handy to keep accessible.

★ Marketing magazines such as *Advertising Age* in the United States and *Marketing* in Canada, are good sources of information on trends and strategies.

★ Other publications such as *Fortune, Success,* business sections of newspapers, and other business magazines sometimes highlight the latest paid research data.

★ Syndicated studies are available in selected industries. These studies are normally enormous in cost and scope, and therefore cost-prohibitive for an independent company to produce. However, the data are normally available at a lower cost to anyone who asks requests it.

- ★ Your own informal polling can be a valuable and accurate source of vital information, provided the sample size is large.
- ★ Customized professional research from companies such as Angus Reid and Market Facts can be well worth the expense when you have a specific proposition that must be tested. Only use this expensive form of research when you have drawn up your plans based on the previous eight research sources mentioned here.

There are five general categories of information you must establish for any venture or brand:
- ★ Your own goals, determined through realistic appraisal of your resources and the tendencies of your audience.
- ★ Your target audience, researched and fully described from both a demographic and psychographic point of view: demographic such as age, sex, geography, household income, home ownership, and so on; psychographic such as preferences, political and social tendencies, lifestyle.
- ★ The benefits to your target audience—e.g., saving money, saving time, showing off, durable performance, and so on. You must fully list all potential benefits against your target audience, then test the audience's response to them.
- ★ The features of your venture or product that support the benefits you've identified, e.g., lowest cost in your industry, fastest processor time, prestige design, and so on. If you have an existing product, obtaining this information is just a matter of inventory. If you are attempting to refine or invent a product or service, you will need to research the response to various features.
- ★ A full list of all special considerations that are relative to your image, including your logo, colors, style, and available photography of stock videography for advertising, and so on.

The Story of Eleanor Wiley

Eleanor Wiley always knew she would succeed. She had raised three children, was happily married for nineteen years, and wanted to go into business. She even knew what business.

In 1984, she prepared her first batch of homemade potato chips for a party. She made them lovingly, seasoning them with her own spice combination. All night, the guests never stopped talking about the chips. Those who knew they were homemade asked, "Why don't you sell them?" and those who didn't asked where they could buy them. Despite many inquiries, Eleanor kept her recipe a secret.

In the Wiley household, Eleanor's chips had become a weekly ritual. Every Saturday she made a fresh batch, and the kids gobbled them up while they were still hot. Her husband, John, teased her constantly about going into the potato chip business, until, one day, she announced that she was going to do just that.

They laughed together, argued a little, and John soon realized that she was serious. He had never seen Eleanor so serious. She began to buy every brand of potato chip. She studied their marketing. She had her family taste-test each one. Still, John wasn't really worried until Eleanor showed him a logo she had designed herself. He teased her that she should not try to go into the design business, but she didn't even crack a smile.

A little frustrated, he asked her what she knew about the potato- chip business. Convenience snacks, she corrected him, and then she told him all she knew in five minutes. She realized she had a lot to learn. John hoped that she would lose interest. She was a qualified high school teacher and could certainly go back to teaching. But every day when he came home, she was at the kitchen table with her laptop computer. She did spreadsheet after spreadsheet. She built a business plan. She visited dozens of convenience stores to ask them what they thought would sell.

The response was lukewarm, until she started touring the shops with a freshly made batch of chips. The stores loved them. She knew she had a hit. She started to ask the stores if they would buy her chips. Most simply declined politely. Her local convenience store manager was a little more direct. "You have to understand. This is big business. We sell more chips than almost anything else. And Hostess and Frito-Lay, well, they sell hundreds of millions of dollars' worth of chips. It's not a cottage business. Brand is really important. Kids and families only want Hostess or Frito-Lay."

Eleanor was despondent but not defeated. She realized she had a lot to learn. Over the next two years, she spent every spare moment polling her neighbors and the local grocery stores. She contacted food industry associations and was surprised at how much information they could offer. She talked to all the friends who would listen—especially those who were in helpful professions: an accountant, a graphic designer, a restaurant owner. She took over the basement and created a large office with competitive potato chip bags tacked up like challenges around her makeshift desk. John was unable to change her mind about pursuing the business, so instead he became her staunchest ally. As an account manager at a local bank, he was able to offer his knowledge of financing.

Together they found out everything there was to know about potato chips. They brainstormed often, trying to figure out a way to differentiate their chip from those of her competitors. Finally, Eleanor hit on an idea one Sunday. "We've done this from the wrong end," she explained. "All that we've learned about the business is that the brands are all the same. There are the mainstream brands all similarly priced. There are the no-names at a slightly lower price. What does that leave?"

Joking, John responded, "A higher price?"

"Exactly," she said. She always remembered that moment when she hit on her idea. She would market upscale. Homemade, country-style potato chips. Her seasoning was light on salt but rich in flavor. She had only one spice mix. Upscale potato chips that were thicker cut, quick fried, and uniquely spiced: she was sure it would work. She would charge more, not less, creating a niche for country-style chips.

Once Eleanor hit upon this idea the plans flowed quickly. She knew almost everything there was to know about convenience foods. She decided that what she needed was a brilliant package design. She went to her graphic-designer friend, to whom she offered a royalty instead of a fee, and within weeks she was in business. She kept the overhead low and started approaching only local stores. They all knew her well by this time. They responded very favorably to the eye-catching packaging and the nifty price point which allowed them to make more money. Still, there were few takers until Eleanor offered her product on consignment. She would make fresh batches every two days, replacing any stock that didn't sell. She purchased a simple bag-sealing press and started distributing her unique country-style chips.

Without exception, every store that agreed to the trial sold out of Eleanor's chips. She was swamped by demand. She couldn't produce them fast enough. With the help of her family and even her neighbors, she began a potato-chip factory in her kitchen. The kids did the packaging in the basement. Her teenage son delivered the chips. The word was spreading almost too quickly.

Finally, with the help of her husband's bank, she received a government-secured loan and bought some higher-volume cooking pots. She hired a part-time cook. She offered her neighbors a commission if anyone got her product into stores that hadn't taken it earlier. Within months she was in the local grocery chain. She developed a business plan that allowed her to expand her business to accommodate the extraordinary demand.

Within two years, Country-Style Chips became the hottest niche snack in Canada. Company revenues went from $45,000 in year one to $650,000 by the end of the year three. Sales doubled the following year. Country-Style Chips were copied by many companies, but Eleanor's idea had caught on and didn't let go. The growth was amazing. John and Eleanor are now full-time vice president and president of the hugely successful Country-Style Chip Co.

Profile

Persona Profile: The Case for Research

Did you know that 71 percent of men shop for fun, just to get out of the house? Or that 46 percent of women believe that an honest person cannot get elected to public office? That 75 percent of consumers believe that big corporations are profit-centered, scandalous, and "out for themselves"? There is nothing that research cannot discover. And this knowledge truly is power for any venture.

Research is vitally important, because the face of society is changing faster than it ever has. The latest statistics from DDB Needham Worldwide's Lifestyle Study indicates that we no longer eat dinner with our families; we all have microwaves and VCRs but we pine for the "old days"; sports cars are growing in popularity and we're driving faster on the road. We are watching less television (believe it or not!) and we're buying more no-name brands. Religion is returning to mass popularity. Disinfectants are important, but messy houses are fine for the majority. We're consciously trying to buy American and we're sharing the household duties with our spouse. Fifty-six percent of us own pets, while an additional 23 percent took in previously owned pets. A majority are in favor of abortion, and a swelling number believe marijuana should be legal.

Interesting trivia or vital information? To marketers, this information is gold. To manufacturers, this information is mandatory. Knowing that 35 percent of the U.S. population is under the age of twenty-five, for instance, dictates major strategy changes for most corporations in or selling to America.

Research shows us where the trends are. While most of us are reducing spending, shopping for deals, and demanding the best price and quality, research indicates specialized habits according to income group. For instance, the middle class with annual incomes of $70,000 or more are spending more than the national average on luxury items; they're still buying expensive cars and fancy clothes and jewelry, while most of us are hanging on to our four-year-old cars and wearing old clothes. Research further shows us that the upper class is shrinking. According to a Mendelson Media Research study, the number of households with over $200,000 in annual income has shrunk from 7.3 percent of the U.S. population in 1992 to only 5.7 percent in 1994.

Research also tells us the ethnic and lifestyle breakdowns of potential markets. Knowing that the entire Asian-American income average is considerably higher than the national average, for example, allows businesses to focus on this growing market. Likewise, understanding that gay men have a much higher discretionary income than heterosexual males allows companies to target this group. And while their preferences are vastly different from the two previous groups mentioned, empty-nesters represent one of the fastest-growing groups that can boast both large disposable incomes and a pleasure-purchase frame of mind.

Most of this research, which represents the meat and potatoes of planning, is published or available through various governments, publications, associations, or market- research companies.

Without research we can only guess. To succeed by guessing requires luck—with odds similar to those of the local lottery. To succeed by planning requires research—and offers odds that any banker would favor.

An Exercise in Research Factoring

Choose the one of the following briefs that contains all five of the important basic elements needed to create a strategy: only one is a complete summary brief with the minimum basic information a marketer would need to get started on a plan. List the missing categories of information in each of the following examples:

Company A

Company A was founded in 1981 to fill a demand for automatic air-freshening systems for public washrooms. It has enjoyed steady growth, averaging 31 percent per year, and it's now at the top of the industry. The company sells mostly to subdistributors, contractors, and wholesalers, and it has a complete mailing list in its database. Company A is the one and only supplier of unique auto-dispensing air-freshening systems. The dispensers pump disinfecting air freshener in steady doses to keep public washrooms smelling fresh. The mechanism is patented, and the inventors hope to license the system to increase their revenues. Their company name is largely unknown, even to the target audience. It's the unique system that sells the product. Marketing consists mostly of a commissioned sales force and collateral support. The principals wish to expand their wholesale network and increase sales.

What important information is missing?

_____

_____

_____

Company B

Company B is a start-up firm set up to market unique electronic window shading systems. The inventors of the systems are the company's principals. They hold patents and trademarks and plan on marketing both wholesale and direct through their toll-free telephone line. They see the largest market as small to medium offices with 50–200 employees and chain restaurants such as Swiss Chalet and Kenny Rogers Chicken. They are also hoping to penetrate the huge consumer market through wholesale agreements. The blind is a motorized system that can be either manually set or programmed by time of day to move automatically. The blind itself is photosensitive, much like tinted glasses, reducing glare and ultraviolet rays even at the lowest tint level. An additional film can be manually deployed to produce a total blackout for presentations. The principals believe that these systems will be hot with computer offices, in which screen glare is a big factor. Both employee comfort and office prestige will be enhanced by their product. Company B has no direct competition and its principals hope to achieve penetration to 4 percent of the total market within two years— producing estimated sales of $55 million. They currently have no special marketing considerations, because they are a start-up.

What important information is missing?

_____

_____

_____

Company C
Company C produces proprietary software for plastic surgeons to assist them in explaining to prospective patients how a procedure will affect their appearance. The system uses video imaging to duplicate the patient's face and graphic technology to overlay new facial features. The computer system is relatively expensive and the technology is not easy to learn. The target audience is plastic surgeons, a relatively fixed market that does not grow rapidly. Only 2 percent of surgeons own imaging systems for their practice, and Company C has two other main competitors. The system is based on a Kritek 8000 computer, upgraded by the company to include optical CD, special software, video interface, and a video camera. The system carries one year of toll-free support and a two-year hardware warranty. On-site installation is included in the price of $18,000.

What important information is missing?

_____

_____

_____

The Most Complete Brief

The most complete profile was Company B. Although any marketer would want more information than is provided here, this brief contains the bare bones:

★ Goals: to achieve penetration of 4 percent of the total market within two years.

★ Target audience: wholesale and direct sale to medium-sized offices of 50–200 and chain restaurants.

★ Benefits to your audience: comfort and office prestige will be enhanced.

★ Features supporting the benefits: automatic tinting windows that keep customers and employees cool and reduce computer screen reflection

★ Special considerations: there are none, because it is a start-up company.

The Incomplete Briefs

Company A was missing three important pieces of the puzzle:

★ Goals: nonspecific goals such as "The principals wish to expand their wholesale network and increase sales" are meaningless to strategic Image-Marketing.

★ Benefits: although the feature is stated as "the one and only supplier of unique auto-dispensing air-freshening systems," no attempt is made to describe why the target audience should care. Do they save money? Keep their customers happy? Motivate staff? Features alone are never enough.

★ Special considerations: there are none stated, but since this is an established company, we should know if we must use a specific logo, corporate colors, or other standards to reinforce the established image of the company.

Company C was missing two important pieces of the brief:

★ Company goals: although we know that only 2 percent of surgeons use Company C equipment, we don't know what objectives the company has. This is the most important element of any planning process.

★ Special considerations.

Persona Tip for Business People

Do you know everything there is to know about your company, your brands, your clients, your prospects, your untapped audiences, your staff, your locality, your government, your economy? It is highly doubtful that any of us knows enough. As Henry Miller once wrote, "In expanding the field of knowledge we but increase the horizon of ignorance." This is a depressing thought for businesses that can profit from knowledge. You can never know it all. Your competitors may be carefully hidden from you. Since business is analogous to war, an ad campaign can become as important as a war campaign. Many top business executives have studied *The Art of War* by Sun Tzu.

You know all you can reasonably learn about competitors, audiences, and your own venture. The more you know—provided you don't squander all your resources on the quest for limitless knowledge—the more likely it is that you can build a Persona Plan that will succeed.

Persona Tip for Entrepreneurs

Research is no less important for the entrepreneur, especially the start-up. What you don't know will kill your venture. Developing a product that is unique but that no one wants is a recipe for failure. The quest to create a product that everyone wants but others already produce is also doomed. Your research will tell you—before you invest your hard-earned money—what will work and what will not.

Persona Tip for Salespeople, Employees, and Personal Persona
Anyone can benefit from research. The salesperson should know her
prospect. The parent should know his child. The employee should
know her company. The same powerful research principles apply to all
areas of life. Lord Chesterfield once wrote in *Letters to His Son*, "If we
don't plant [knowledge] while we are young, it will give us no shade
when we grow old." The quest for knowledge never stops. From
research and knowledge come plans that cannot fail.

The Independence Factor

▼

*Persona must live. You must give birth to a perfect child,
nurture your child, educate your child, and then allow the persona
to live free of parental encumbrances.*

Definition

A correctly constructed Persona Plan, based on research,
is only the beginning—the birth. Once your persona is born, you must
develop, expand, and elaborate, until the persona can function
on its own. Nurturing allows growth in your objectives. Allow your
persona to live independently of its creators. Become an employee of
your creation, rather than the founder of the venture.
Let your personified venture grow equity in its identity that is not
dependent on your personal interference.

What It Means

*"...freedom cannot exist without
economic security and independence."*
Franklin D. Roosevelt

Microsoft does not need the support of Bill Gates. His high-profile "richest-man-in America" status has nothing to do with Microsoft's corporate status. The creators of the Apple Macintosh have largely gone their own way, leaving behind a spectacularly successful culture that changed the world.

Even if you are a start-up, even if you are personally famous in your industry, you must treat your personified venture as an independent child. This child must be allowed to grow on its own. You must be content to be the proud parent of a brilliant child instead of the brilliant parent.

The Independence Factor is an important final step in your Persona Planning. Everything you do must be directed toward creating a totally unique and independent persona for your venture. You cannot achieve the status of Microsoft or Macintosh by making your will and your name more important than those of your ventures. Certainly, after your spectacular success, you can step in and claim all the credit for your amazing brainchild. But, for now, put your ego aside and build an entity in your venture.

There are two types of immortality that are certain: your children will carry on long after you pass, and your venture will thrive for many decades after you retire, as long as you build a strong persona.

This is why we advocate the naming and incorporation of any business. Incorporating makes the new persona a legal entity that really does have its own life. Name your endeavor, develop a logo, develop a full persona—then let it have its own life.

Our own companies, Two Dimensions Inc. and The Persona Principle Inc., thrive independently of their founders. We still own all of the shares in our companies, and we still profit from our companies, but the companies have outgrown any dependence on us. We didn't make the mistake of naming our Advertising Agency "Armstrong, Yu, and Associates"—a common strategy for naming ad agencies. Even though our reputation and experience were the main reason our earlier clients hired Two Dimensions Inc., we knew that the company had to be more than the sum of its parts. The corporation has a mind—our wonderful staff. It has a body—our equipment, building, portfolio of past work, and other tools of the trade. It has friends—our valued clients. It has critics—our respected competition. It grows, year after year, like any human being—growing in experience, knowledge, and value. Two Dimensions Inc. no longer needs Armstrong and Yu to help it grow. We could easily retire, enjoying the fruits of our hard work in comfortable leisure. Two Dimensions is like a growing person, now an adult that makes its own decisions, mistakes, triumphs, and relationships.

If you can't make this conceptual leap—understanding that your venture is a persona separate from your own and that it must grow and be independent of you—then you are condemning your company to being only as good as you are personally.

Be the good parent: bring your child up in the best way you can— teaching morals, creativity, values, survival, independence—then step aside and let your venture have its own life. You'll become the proud parent.

Independence Factoring Techniques

Most of the techniques described in the Persona Codes are ways to build the independence of your corporation. Consistently following the 8 Persona Factors plus 88 Persona Codes will not only make your venture grow financially, it will also help your venture build a strong identity. Here are some basic techniques:

★   Be sure to name your venture something other than your own name.

★   Incorporate your venture or trademark your brand.

★   Create a logo.

★   Always refer to the venture by its name, deemphasizing the founders.

★   Write a mission statement for your venture, and let the company live it.

★   Develop a company culture. This step is easiest when you introduce new employees to it from the beginning. Let the culture evolve and grow.

★   Avoid any personal vanity statements, especially in your marketing. Avoid appearing in your own advertising, unless you are already a hero or expert who is known to your audience. If you are not known, don't try to build your reputation at the expense of that of your ventures. Hiring professional talent for your marketing is an important Persona technique. Just as you should hire the best graphic designers for your logo, the best advertising agency for your ads, and the best staff for your company, you must also have the best spokesperson for your venture. Actors always appear more credible and confident in an ad than the founder and president.

The Story of Doug Forberg and Jason Salson

Doug Forberg and Jason Salson had made a good living for twelve years, but neither was satisfied with their level of success. Forberg, Salson and Associates was a reliable, conservative architectural design firm that had shown marginal growth. The firm was respected but not well known. The bank loved the company's conservatism, but prospective clients didn't flock to their doors. Their staff and clients were happy but Forberg and Salson were not.

Forberg, Salson and Associates was a solid company with nine architects and two support staff employees. They had an attractive downtown office that casually emphasized their talents. The atmosphere in the office was sophisticated and corporate. When prospects visited FSA, they were pleasantly impressed.

Doug and Jason were restless. They saw their competitors growing. They saw their main archrivals landing all the big contracts. They were left with the small redesigns and renovation jobs. They tendered bids for and lost at least a dozen major contracts a year. Their niche had become the small-budget renovation. They felt they were much better than their reputation allowed—they were brilliant architects—but their portfolio of work only reflected the niche they had accidentally fallen into. They had no spectacular large-budget design project to show off.

In the twelfth year of their business, Doug and Jason were galvanized into action by the loss of a client they had worked with for eight years.

Discreet but angry, Doug called the client and asked the reason for their dismissal. He was not surprised by the answer, but he was bitterly disappointed. "We've outgrown FSA, Doug. I'm sorry. We need a full-service firm with experience in large buildings." Doug tried to keep his voice calm as he asked why the client thought FSA couldn't handle the bigger job. The answer to this question was a surprise. "Well, it's simple. We know that FSA is you and Jason. You're both talented designers, but this project will require many talented designers. The two of you wouldn't be able to handle it."

Doug and Jason met for drinks at their favorite neighborhood bar. They were both smarting over the loss. Their client had given them over $2 million in billings over the past few years. They snapped at each other, argued awhile, and finally decided that the client was right. If they wanted to grow, they couldn't promote themselves as the principal designers. After all, they had nine other top designers.

"The problem is our name, isn't it?" Doug asked between beers. "I mean, our company has our name. But who are we?" Jason didn't agree and they argued hotly about Doug's growing conviction that they should change the firm's name. Jason maintained that changing the name would blow away any value they had built in their name. "Think about it, Jason," Doug urged. "Almost all architectural firms have names that sound like ours. How can clients remember us?" Despite Jason's persistent objections, Doug won in the end with a curt "As long as we are Forberg, Salson and Associates, we'll always be known as just the two of us."

They went from arguing to brainstorming. The bar's paper napkins filled up with dozens of name ideas. As Doug and Jason drank more, the ideas got wilder, and they became more excited about finding the right name. They decided that the most important element of the name was to emphasize that there were many designers in their firm. They agreed that whatever name they came up with would be appended by the word Group. This made their quest easier. The word The naturally had to precede the name if it was appended by Group. So far, they knew their new name would be The ——— Group.

It was three weeks before Doug and Jason could agree on the right word. Finally, they decided that the missing element in their business was excitement. They needed big, innovative projects. So they decided their name would reflect their goals. FSA became "The Innovation Group." At first, neither was happy with their name. They had agreed through compromise, not by inspiration. But it grew on them.

They developed an aggressive plan to launch the new name. They briefed their staff and hired a graphic designer to create a brilliant new logo and create an impressive capabilities brochure. They did not mention FSA in any of their new promotions, but they assumed the benefits of FSA. When customers asked how long they had been in business, they honestly responded twelve years. When prospects asked for a customer list, they provided the list compiled under FSA. They deemphasized anything that would make them appear to be a small operation. They reprinted all their stationery with their impressive new logo.

The results were not instantaneous. Although prospects were impressed by the colorful brochure, many existing clients assumed they had been bought out. The receptionist stumbled for a few weeks on the new name, but soon it became a persona. The firm started to do things differently. They redecorated the office, creating a more "innovative" interior. They knocked down a wall in the boardroom, eliminating an office but creating an impressive meeting room. They implemented some of their more ingenious architectural ideas in their own building.

At the end of their twelve years in business, the firm finally landed its first major contract. Three years later, they had tripled in size. Most of the employees don't even remember the name Forberg, Salson and Associates. They are The Innovation Group.

Persona Profile: The Independence Culture

Which of the following names do you think of when you are considering a ready-to-drink iced tea?

★ Ssips
★ Turkey Hill
★ Snapple

Most would pick Snapple. Snapple owns 31.3 percent of the ready-to-drink iced-tea market, while Ssips and Turkey Hill own only 1.4 percent and 0.9 percent, respectively.

When you think of a toothpaste, what name comes to you first?

★ Mentadent
★ Rembrandt
★ Ultra Brite
★ Crest

You likely answered Crest. With a gigantic $430.4 million in sales, it owns the top of mind in toothpaste.

For garbage bags, which brand is on the tip of your tongue?

★ Glad
★ Good Sense
★ Ruffies Color Scents

You probably chose Glad.

Which brand is your intimate friend when you think of toilet paper?

★ Coronet
★ M.D.

★ Charmin
Charmin, of course.

For diapers, we think first of Pampers. For adult incontinence, we think of Depend. Storage bags are Ziploc and pasta in a can is good old Chef Boy-Ar-Dee.

Why do these brands stand out in the top of our minds? Is it because we have been bombarded with year upon year of advertising? Or is it because we have been consistently fed a regular diet of the same message?

As important as ad spending is to reaching an audience, the numbers indicate that consistency is many times more important. In almost all of the above examples, ad spending by the number two and number three in each market was equal to or higher than the number one. The most important factor is the culture of the product. "The Man from Glad" and "Chef Boy-Ar-Dee" are personas that are remembered and stay in the mind. They become part of our collective conscious. The top 200 brands, from number one AT&T to number 200 Duracell, have built a culture we can all relate to. The brands all have distinct identities of their own. Their personas have been nurtured through consistent image and steady advertising.

In most cases, we don't know or care who made the product. Who knows that Pampers are from Procter & Gamble? Or that Ziploc bags are made by Dow Chemical Company? Did you know that Häagen-Dazs ice cream comes from an American company?

The only factor that has any value is the persona of the brand. Advertising spending alone can never displace these mega-brand personas. The top brand success stories are always brands that have a life of their own. We don't know or care who makes the product. We only know the culture of the product.

An Exercise in Independence Factoring

The Naming Game
by James McKinnon

> Copywriter James McKinnon of Two Dimensions Inc., who has personally developed many powerful company names, wrote this concise and helpful guide to the important art of naming. After you read his tips, he challenges you with The Naming Game.

"What's in a name?" Juliet wondered after finding out her Romeo had the wrong one. "That which we call a rose by any other name would smell as sweet," she went on philosophically. Her conclusion? If the name doesn't suit, change it!

And so believed Marilyn Monroe, star, icon, goddess. Why didn't she stay plain old Norma Jean Baker? Because somebody in Hollywood, where they know a lot about image, thought that Marilyn was sexier and the alliterative Monroe smoother and the whole thing more marketable. Were they right? Seems so.

Marion Michael Morrison—lots of alliteration there—must have agreed when those same Hollywood types told him he was going nowhere in the movies until he dropped the androgyny and became John Wayne, he-man and hero. Now he's in the movie star pantheon, and Marion Michael Morrison is in parentheses.

Writers know how important names are for revealing character. Dickens was especially good with a name. Think of Scrooge. The word now means what it sounds like—we use it to characterize mean, money-grubbing old men, just as Dickens did. Demagogues, too, know when to change a name. Would the Russian masses rally to Iosif Vissarionovich Dzhugashvilli? He didn't think they would, so he became Stalin. Schicklegruber didn't have much of a ring to it either, but Hitler was a name with terrifying power.

We know that a name can be powerful socially, opening doors if it's a "good" name, closing them if it's not. Choosing a name, then, is one of your most important tasks when you decide to go into business.

Indeed, the right name can be a big boost to your business, while the wrong name can sink you.

The big question is, therefore, What kind of name should you use?

The answer is, it depends. It depends on who you are, what kind of business or venture you're naming, who you want to reach, and a lot of other factors. Here are a few of the possibilities.

The Family Name

Some of the greatest names in the history of commercial enterprise are nothing more than the name of the inventor or founder of the company: Ford, DuPont, Rolls-Royce, Boeing, Gillette. These mighty names have built equity over many years and have now become inseparable from the products their companies manufacture.

Unless your name is Rockefeller, Kennedy, or Armani, it probably doesn't have the same clout, and the world has changed since those genius inventors and entrepreneurs started their empires. Still, a lot of law firms, architectural firms, and engineering firms go this traditional naming route. The danger? Being lost in a sea of commas and ampersands—Bradley, Cooper, Dickson, Gallagher, & Meredith; Harroldson, McKinley, Foster, Josephs, & Zelunka; etc., etc., & etc.

An important exception occurs when an unusual family name, whose very strangeness or humor makes it stand out, gives you an angle with which to differentiate yourself—e.g., Orville Redenbacher, Smucker's, Reese's Pieces.

Our rule of thumb: don't use your own name, unless there's a really good reason to do so.

The Acronym

Acronyms have become annoyingly pervasive in today's world of causes, strange diseases, and interest groups. There's MADD (Mothers Against Drunk Driving), SAD (Seasonal Affective Disorder), GATT (General Agreement on Tariffs and Trade), NAFTA (North American Free Trade Agreement), PETA (People for the Ethical Treatment of Animals), and so on ad infinitum.

Still, the acronym is a good choice when you're dealing with something complex, technical, and difficult to name with existing words. The best acronyms actually become words in their own right —who remembers that RADAR stands for Radio Detecting and Ranging or that SCUBA means Self-Contained Underwater Breathing Apparatus?

I recently needed to name a sophisticated technical process for making replicas, at any size, of any object or land form. The process involves stereoscopic photography, telemetry, and equipment most people could never relate to. I called it SMART: Stereoscopic Mapping and Rescaling Technology. The clients now have a handy, nonthreatening name for their complex, incomprehensible-to-the-layman process.

The Invented Name

Invented names have some pretty good credentials. Everybody knows what nylon is. How many know what it *really* is: polyhexamethyleneadipamide? Any wonder they made up the name? Or how about Häagen-Dazs? Looks foreign, doesn't it? Must be better than the domestic stuff, right? A lot of consumers apparently agree. The ice cream is strictly U.S.-manufactured, but the name gives it an exotic appeal.

A lot of invented names are pretty flimsy, though. Would you want your driveway paved with DESIGNCRETE, no matter how decorative and long-lasting the job? And, of course, many invented names are nothing more than parts of other words stuck together, especially in the hi-tech industries: ACCUTEL, COMPTECH IMAGTECH, TELECOM. These names work well enough, but there's such a sameness to them! Much more friendly and human are names such as Macintosh, with its familiar little apple logo.

The Descriptive Name

A good name can clearly and succinctly describe, or at least suggest, the nature of your product or business. Obviously, if you're in the truck rental business or appliance repairs, you're going to say so in your name. "Bill's Truck Rentals" is good enough if your name's Bill and you rent trucks.

But what if you're starting up a consultancy—say, fund raising for the arts by direct mail? What do you call yourself? John Doe Consulting? Doe and Associates? What do these names mean to anyone? Wy not try something a little more descriptive, even if it's not flashy, like "John Doe Direct Mail Fund-Raising"? At least it's clear what you do and you won't be getting time-wasting calls from people looking for help with their funeral arrangements.

"Speedy Muffler King" works well. It says what the company does and at the same time it identifies its main benefit: speed.

The Humorous Name

Humorous names sometimes occur inadvertently, in which case they can be embarrassing or worse. My personal favorite: a Chinese funeral home in Toronto with the delightfully optimistic moniker Wing On Funeral Chapel. A close second, along the same thematic lines, is Dr. Coffin, the mortician. Would you want to learn the complex and dangerous skill of driving a car at a school with the word Lucky in its name?

When used intentionally, humorous names have a couple of advantages. They can make you stand out in the Yellow Pages and they appeal to a certain audience. Naturally you should use humor judiciously, keeping your target audience very tightly in focus.

There's a pool hall I know, grandly named the Academy of Spherical Arts. And the company "Rent A Wife" has chosen an eye-catching name; it's a maid service.

The important thing about naming is to choose something you can live with for a long time, something that won't look silly or dated a year or two later, and something that really represents your uniqueness to your specific audience.

Here's a little exercise in naming. Match the business to the name. See what happens when you mismatch.

❏ beauty parlor	a. Breaking Away
❏ mortuary	b. The Last Roundup
❏ aftertheater café	c. Chaps
❏ singles bar	d. Eliza's
❏ bed and breakfast	e. Elle
❏ dude ranch	f. Happy Acres
❏ marriage counselor	g. Morrison Brothers
❏ flower shop	h. Curtains

Now try your own. Invent a name for the following ventures:
★ A financial counseling service for seniors
★ A pet-sitting service
★ A new line of business and account management software
★ A new cookie for adults
★ A computer consulting firm offering to help existing companies become fully computerized and/or upgrade

Persona Tip for Business People

The most important review you can make of your business involves all of your identifying factors. Have you captured top-of-mind status in your target audience? If not, why not? How many of your prospects know your company or brand name? Nothing is more important than name recognition. Your salespeople have a tough credibility sell if they cold-call a prospect who has never heard of you. Is your company name easy to say and remember? Without recall, you'll never achieve top-of-mind status. And you'll never achieve recall without an easy name. Is your logo simple, clear, impactful? All of these elements affect the visible manifestations of the identity of the living creature that is your venture. Encourage a culture among your employees. Involve your clients in this culture through marketing. Do everything you can to separate your venture from your competition, so that your venture lives in your audience's mind.

Persona Tip for Entrepreneurs

Nothing is as vital to a start-up venture's success as the name. In advertising, there is one requirement that is universal, regardless of which agency you hire, who you target, what media you use, or which marketing consultant you listen to. Every ad ever produced must incorporate the name of the venture. Without a name, you cannot achieve recall in your audience. Without recall, you will have no business.

Develop a proper Persona Plan before your name. The act of creating a culture for your company—through your Plan—will lead to the development of a powerful name. Recently, our client CCNS, in the middle of a Persona Inventory, discovered their own name. The inventory indicated that CCNS was not a memorable name. They had a solid, profitable business, but prospects had trouble with the name—especially since one of their competitors has an almost identical name. In the middle of our Persona Inventory, the president offered, "we're The Information Place" as the description of what the company did. In fact, CCNS is the largest source of public information searches and registrations in Canada. The Information Place. It became part of the name. To retain the equity in the original name, the company decided to revise the name to be CCNS — The Information Place. The culture changed almost immediately. The staff, answering the phones "CCNS—The Information Place," realized that their focus had changed. CCNS was now positioned as the only company in Canada that could search or register *all* types of information.

Whether you conduct a full Persona Inventory or not, spend as much time on developing or improving your name as it takes. Days, weeks, or even months of your time is a small investment to make for your future success.

Persona Tip for Salespeople, Employees, and Personal Persona

The impact of the Independence Factor is not limited to corporations. In different ways, the persona of a salesperson, employee, or individual takes on its own identity. The persona in the office is not the same persona the family knows at home. She may have the same ethical or social values, but her presentation is different. An employee should actively encourage separate images, although not to the point of schizophrenia. The professional persona is a vital tool to help you achieve your goals. You should assume that character when you are at work, but leave it at behind when you go home.

Even in interpersonal situations, our persona changes in different atmospheres. The Jane Doe who is so polite and courteous with work associates can become the mad party animal at the local pub. The John Smith who is the loving father at home might be the forceful speaker at a political debate. The various personas we assume are not emotionally dangerous or confusing. We are tailoring our presentations to those receiving our message, always with the sole objective of selling our idea. Knowing that we automatically assume different personas can lead to improved success through formal Persona Planning. You can always inventory and plan your presentation—particularly in situations in which you are motivated by an important issue.

PART FOUR

THE 88
PERSONA CODES

▼

" The image of myself which I try to create in my own mind in order that I may love myself is very different from the image which I try to create in the minds of others in order that they may love me."
W. H. Auden

The Dyer's Hand

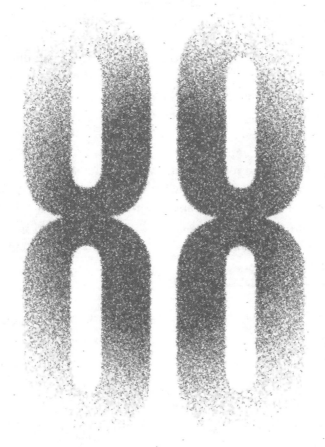

The 8 Persona Factors are the roots of the Persona Tree. The 88 Persona Codes are the branches. These are the building blocks of your success persona. These Persona Codes of Conduct offer you advice that is proven through years of marketing practice. Think of these as business and marketing maxims. All 88 of these codes are incorporated into the Persona Inventory and Planning Guide as mathematical formulas. Each of these codes has a direct impact on your business.

Learn these codes, understand them, use them. If you choose to conduct a full Persona Inventory, understanding the codes will make the process clearer. If you choose to incorporate Persona informally into your venture, try to follow as many of these principles as you can.

Our tests with many clients have proven that consistent and precise application of these principles will guarantee results.

Some Persona Codes highlight subjects already discussed, such as imaging, impact, frequency, and so on. The Persona Codes emphasize all of the rules of good imaging, including some mentioned in earlier parts of this book. The codes are the formal statements of these maxims. Some codes are very similar in idea. For example, the Code of Twos and the Code of First Mind both talk about the important subject of narrow positioning, although from different points of view. In cases in which two codes discuss a similar theme from different perspectives, you should pay particular attention to the central ideas.

1—Code of Imaging

Your prime directive—above all other marketing considerations—is support of your visible persona. If you have a Persona Plan, follow it strictly. Whatever a client or prospective client might see must be perfect and planned. Your visible image is important to impact. Impact is important to visibility. Set standards for any aspect of your venture that is visible to your audience.

Mini Persona Profile: Imaging Through Logos

Logos and names are the first visible manifestations of a company that your audience is likely to see. In an extensively researched study of logos by The Schecter Group, it was found that logos can both enhance and damage image. Kentucky Fried Chicken scored the highest, with a 24 percent increase in brand- image response. This means that the audience's reaction to KFC improved by 24 percent when showed the logo of Colonel Sanders over just seeing the brand name. Federal Express, on the other hand, suffered a 25 percent loss of brand-image response when their logo was shown. The new FedEx logo is a straightforward type treatment with a nearly invisible arrow hidden in the E. This and other studies prove that a properly executed logo can enhance image, while a poorly executed logo can do severe damage. Remember, your prime directive is image first, so don't cheap out on your logo!

2—Code of Rationales

Everything you do must have a raison d'être. Never undertake any endeavor, of any size, without a written rationale. Never create a name, a brand, or a short-term or long-term strategy without complete and irrefutable justification. Conduct extensive research before preparing a plan. You want to know—before you commit your resources—whether or not you can succeed.

3—Code of Playing Hard-to-Get

Get in the habit of saying no to everyone. No gives you strength. Playing hard to get gets people to want you even more. Say maybe instead of yes. If you are going to say yes, hesitate. Don't seem anxious. The way you use this code depends on your positioning. If your persona presents an inexpensive alternative, you will not say no as quickly as you would if you were positioned as the best, most expensive alternative. The best always stand firm.

Mini Persona Profile: Playing Hard-to-Get On-Line

America OnLine recently announced that its in-demand on-line service will accept advertising. The catch is that it is offering only a one-year package that costs $300,000. Advertising agencies, who have been waiting for an opportunity to get on-line, are already complaining that it is too expensive. But America OnLine is using the hard-to-get strategy, insisting on the one-year fee. It's in a position to do this because it's popular with users, and advertisers are anxious to get into the system. This strategy positions the on-line service on the high end. If it had wanted to corner the low end, it would have offered multiple, cost-variable packages.

4—Code of Religion

Make your persona an evangelical cause, and treat the persona with reverence. Do strict penance if you accidentally break any commandment. You must inspire enthusiasm in your staff, your prospects and your clients. Evangelism means you must live, breath, sleep, and dream your venture's culture. Without this kind of commitment, you can achieve only mediocrity.

5—Code of First Mind

Always be first. If you can't be first, invent a niche in which you can be first. It is important that you be first in the mind of your target audience. You gain little credibility by claiming you are fifth in your market. You must position your persona to be number one in a segment in which you can meet your objectives—even if you have to invent that segment. Many great success stories have come from this drive to be number one. For example, the Uncola was created to overcome Coca-Cola's number one status. As a result, 7UP, the Uncola, is number one in the clear soft-drink category that it invented.

6—Code of Exposure

It is never enough to be first or best. You must expose your claim constantly to your target audience. The best in quality is not always the winner. Only the best in the audience's mind can claim this title. Quality helps, but only if everyone is aware of it. Never stop telling your audience your message. Commit at least 5 percent of your revenues to making sure your audience remains exposed.

Mini Persona Profile: Television Exposure

Zenith, once number two in the TV market, has dropped to number three from lack of advertising. In 1994 It spent only $1.8 million, a tiny percentage of its revenues, to reach its audience. Meanwhile, Magnavox has doubled its share, leaping into second place by spending $18 million on marketing. This was accomplished in spite of Zenith's reputation for quality and innovation. Since these benefits are hidden from its audience, Zenith cannot build on them.

7—Code of Creativity

To overcome the invisibility barrier, develop your creativity. Brainstorm until you have only original ideas. Hire consultants to offer you brilliant creative ideas for your advertising. Settle only for the most creative of logos, advertising, marketing, and public relations. Be sure that the creative executions conform exactly to your Persona Plan.

Mini Persona Profile: Frosted Mini Wheats

Kellogg's runaway advertising success story was Frosted Mini Wheats. Brand sales doubled, between 1990 and 1994, to $260 million, largely as the result of a strikingly creative ad campaign. The advertising shows an adult who extols the virtues of whole wheat suddenly turning into a kid who loves the frosted side. The clever special effects, humor, and clear message to the "kid in you" are driving the success of this brand.

8—Code of Memory

Your persona must be easy to remember. One word is twice as powerful as two. Two is twice as powerful as three. The most powerful memory number is one. Any proposition that must be explained with more words will not be remembered. Any positioning statement over five words is obscure. Go for short messages: overnight delivery, flame-broiled burgers, quietest automobile (these messages are owned, respectively, by FedEx, Burger King, and Lexus).

9—Code of Body Language

Everything you do and say affects your persona. Always appear true to your persona in your clothing, your habits, and your speech. Body language is one of the most powerful influencers. This may mean you need a formal dress code for your company (or an informal one, if that is your company's character). Prospects and clients should not be confused by too many different styles of image.

Avoid negative persona mannerisms, such as crossed arms, crossed legs, rapid eye blinking, and other unfriendly body language signals. Always speak clearly and concisely. Don't put your prospect to sleep with long-winded pitches. Never interrupt a prospect, and when you are talking, be sure to pause often to see if the other person wants to speak.

10—Code of the Package

Packaging, in all its manifestations, is one of the most important Persona elements. The package is the vehicle through which you are perceived. If you are the manufacturer of a product, how you package it will determine how much impact and credibility you will gain on the store shelf. If you are a consultant, how you package yourself will determine how seriously you are taken. Minimizing or eliminating packaging may help consumers realize you are socially conscious. Creating a wild splash with your packaging can give a start-up venture the thrust it needs. Packaging must be strategic and targeted at your specific audience.

11—Code of the Race

Race into the mind. Never walk. Explosions of messages are more valuable than quiet, steady marketing. You must be the first—so explode a bomb, not a firecracker.

12—Code of Goals

Nothing should ever be undertaken without a goal. No goals means no success—and no measure of success. No venture has a right to exist, and no Persona Plan can exist, without specific goals.

13—Code of Barriers

Do not erect any barriers between yourself and your target audience. For every handler you hire, every department you create, you lose important input. The more barriers you erect, the less power you have. Automatic phone attendants are a barrier. Secretaries are a barrier, even to your staff. Remember that you need input from employees, clients, prospects, suppliers, and competitors. Don't cut yourself off.

14—Code of Ownership

You must own something. Usually it is a word. Sometimes a thing. But you must own it completely. It must be shared with no one. This is an important marketing principle. If you are currently number three in your niche, modify your niche so you can be number one. Become the first no-tube television. Don't compete where you can't rule. Take your basic offering and modify it so that it is superior or different. Or, if you are selling a consumer product that cannot be differentiated based on quality—such as peas—create a unique character, such as the Jolly Green Giant. Whether you own a word a character or an idea, it must be yours and no one else's.

15—Code of the Hero

Regardless of your niche, you must be a hero in it. A common psychographic of all people is their love of romance, heroes, and spectacle. Work spectacle and heroism into your persona in credible doses. This suggestion does not mean you should create a Hero Persona. All ventures should have an element of heroism, of romance. The ball-bearings manufacturer can be a hero to the machinist. Nike can be a hero to the high school student.

16—Code of Character

As an early step in your Persona Plan, create a fictional character that exactly expresses your persona. Describe the sex, looks, personality, race, clothing, and language and then romanticize the image. Finally, become the character. This is not just an exercise. It is a thoughtful way to define your goals, your perceptions, and your audience. Are you Sherlock Holmes or Matlock? Dennis the Menace or Superman? Better yet, invent a character and use this character in your marketing. The character must express your product. Characters such as the Pillsbury Dough Boy and the Man from Glad can become icons if marketed correctly, helping you to grow brands. Whether you use your character in your marketing or not, add characteristics to your persona. They will help you develop your venture or your corporate culture.

17—Code of Service

You can't replace a customer. No client is dispensable. Even the customer who is totally unreasonable and infuriates your staff is valuable. *Advertising Age* magazine wrote that the average cost of obtaining a new customer is six times that of keeping an existing customer.

Implement the highest level of customer service. Take your client's side over your staff's. As valuable as your staff is, your clients are worth more. If it costs you $200 to solve a customer's problem, it's still less than the cost of obtaining a new client. The Code of Service should be framed over your desk to remind you each day how vital each and every client is to your success.

18—Code of Inventory

The first step in building a persona is to inventory all that you—or your product—have now: your desires, skills, weaknesses, and strengths. Every time you add a skill or asset, update your inventory. It is also useful to inventory your competition and your prospects. A classic example of the power of inventory was the brilliant strategic move by SmithKline Beecham. Its Tums brand had been tied with Rolaids until it took stock and decided to differentiate the two products. It added calcium to its antacid formula and began heavy marketing that pointed out the difference. Tums soared past Rolaids and now dominates the market with a 21.2 percent share over Rolaids's 10.7 percent.

Do a formal or informal inventory or update at least every quarter. This routine allows you to measure changes and recognize opportunities. To be able to solve problems as SmithKline Beecham did, you must know all there is to know about your product, your competition, and your audience. If you use the Persona Inventory, you'll have actual numbers that precisely move up or down, indicating exactly where you should act. Completing a quarterly inventory will enable you to correct problems before they become too serious. The act of asking questions and discovering answers will teach you unexpected things about yourself, your venture, your audience, and your associates.

19—Code of Risks
If you are unwilling to take risks, you will never progress. Eventually you will fade. Analyze risks, then take brave steps toward your goals. Calculated risks sprinkle the path to success. Without risk you can never be first. If you are not first, you cannot sell. Risk takers capture success. Of course, extensive research and planning minimize risk.

20—Code of Continuity
Inconsistency is damaging to persona. Campaigns have more power than single ads. With constant competition for your target audience's mind, it is crucial that you never confuse this audience by being inconsistent in any of your messages. The Man from Glad must always wear white. The Pillsbury Dough Boy must always giggle. These characters cannot be changed without damaging the equity invested in them.

21—Code of Horn Blowing
Never stop telling your audience how good you are. Blow your own horn while avoiding both arrogance and modesty. Make sure your horn has only one sound, so the listener knows who it is. Make sure the sound is pleasant. Your approach to publicity must be positive, consistent, and in perfect sync with your persona.

Mini Persona Profile: The Benetton Publicity Nightmare

Probably the most often quoted cliché of marketing is the most erroneous: "Any publicity is good publicity."

Many companies have failed through this approach. Negative image is never good publicity—no matter how many people the message reaches. It makes you visible, but not visible with the persona you wish to project. This "scream until you are noticed" technique is completely at odds with the science of Persona.

The inherent weakness in public relations strategies is the lack of control. You cannot guarantee or even influence what is written or spoken about you or your venture using this haphazard marketing maxim. You have as much chance of being damaged or ruined by this approach as you do of becoming well-known. The Code of Horn Blowing demands positive and consistent image. In other words: *Only good publicity is good publicity.*

Perhaps the clearest example of using high-profile negative publicity in advertising was the well-known Benetton poster campaign. Luciano Benetton would have argued hotly against our position on negative publicity. Benetton used negative social issues to draw attention to the company. For a while, the spectacle worked well. Famous posters depicting the most horrifying social problems contributed to Benetton's notoriety. The association with negative issues allowed for rapid franchise growth.

Unfortunately, there is no equity in these attention-demanding techniques. As it grew, Benetton was forced to create more and more shocking images to stay in the public eye. Images of an AIDS patient and Palestinian refugees have grabbed headlines everywhere—and turned away shoppers by the hundreds of thousands. Sales dropped, and operating profits have slipped 5 percent to $244 million. Several owners of Benetton franchises are suing Benetton over the impact of these negative PR ventures, claiming lost sales. In 1995, when other fashion giants were surging forward in sales, Benetton was plummeting. The controversial campaign has been dropped, replaced by a too-late image-building TV advertising campaign. But the damage is done.

Negative Image-Equity is very difficult to reverse. Benetton's rapid growth—based on "scream and be noticed" PR—has built no foundation for long-term growth. Screaming for attention requires that you scream louder and louder to stay in the spotlight. This is why the Benetton campaign moved from relatively high profile but not-too-disturbing to shocking imagery. The gruesome image campaign kept it high profile but contributed to its downfall. The lesson is that only positive horn blowing has long-term growth value.

22—Code of the Dark Half

Never show your Dark Half. Everyone has a dark side—a prejudice, a temper—but you should never reveal it in front of a client. If you feel you cannot control your temper, stay home. Do not allow mood to affect persona. Similarly, never show the dark side of your product unless it cannot be hidden. If you cannot hide the problem, be sure you are the one who tells the world about it.

Mini Persona Profile: The Pentium Disaster

In your inventory of your weaknesses, never forget the competition. In early 1995, IBM blew the whistle on computer-chip competitor Intel. Once in 27,000 years, Intel's Pentium chip could be mathematically inaccurate in large calculations. However, Intel, which owns 75 percent of the market, kept silent. Whether out of arrogance or fear, the computer giant damaged its hard-earned blue-chip equity by zipping its collective lip. Until this disaster, Intel's customers assumed its product was of the highest standard. Now they know Intel is flawed. Instead of recalling the product, Intel stubbornly insisted that an occurrence of the problem was improbable. Consumers responded with fury. How could they trust a company that could make a processor that made math errors?

The mistake Intel made was losing sight of the competition. Your rivals will always be the first to reveal your Dark Half.

23—Code of Complainers

The only person who should hear your complaints is yourself. Complainers are weak and appear weak. Excuses are never allowed —even if you have a good one. Avoid complaining about your competition in your marketing. MCI made this mistake in a 1994 campaign that shouted "Shame on you, AT&T." MCI's whiny ads only served to contribute to its rival's success: AT&T signed up 1 million subscribers that year, including many who had originally defected to MCI for promised discounts. Complaining never works, and it may irreparably damage your persona.

24—Code of the Collective Conscious

Do not try to contradict the "collective consciousness" of your audience. If your customers believe "made in Japan" is better than "made in the U.S.," you waste energy contradicting the Collective— even if they are completely wrong. Find your own unique message that does *not* contradict any Collective norms. You may be faster, but can you make your audience believe it? You may be longer-lasting, but they may never accept it. Find a way to appeal to the Collective Conscious. Never contradict it.

Mini Persona Profile: A Conscious Shift

In 1986, BMW was the yuppie car of choice. Almost everyone who made three times their age in thousands of dollars annually owned one. But BMW had to rethink its strategy when society shifted attitudes. We moved from the "greed decade" to the "green decade." We no longer want prestige. We want value and quality. Suddenly, BMW advertising began stressing German engineering and quiet competence. Abruptly, new models with lower prices were introduced. And BMW has succeeded where other yuppie products have failed.

25—Code of Patience

Never expect success. If you are sure you did everything right, if you researched and planned until nothing could go wrong, then you probably believe you will succeed. If you completed a Persona Plan correctly and if your goals are realistic, you have a statistical likelihood of succeeding. Venturists often fail in their inability to wait. They spend all their reserves on their plan, assuming instant response, and go bankrupt before their customers can respond. Building equity is a slow process. It takes at least two years on average for a Persona Plan to succeed. It takes two years for a start-up venture to prove it can work. Patience is mandatory. Persona does not offer the fast track to success—it just offers the surest path.

26—Code of Weakness

You must not show any weakness—not even the slightest weakness. Demonstrate only your strengths. Usually the qualities of your strengths and virtues will overcome any doubts your audience may have. But give them the slightest hint of a weakness, and you'll never recover. Strategically, if you can't hide your weakness, you should try turning it into a strength. If your weakness is only a weakness to one audience, find a new audience who might not notice or mind the weakness. Volkswagen mastered this strategy in the sixties when it advertised its funny-looking car the Bug. "Think small," it offered, at a time when cars were growing giant tail fins. If you can't beat them, don't join them. Instead, find a place where your weakness is considered an advantage.

27—Code of Impact

Without impact, you will not be noticed. With too much impact you won't be credible. Such is the fine balance master advertisers must maintain. Shocking ads only work for audiences who don't mind being shocked. Sega's current series of bizarre advertising appeals directly and successfully to its younger audience. If it targeted an older audience, sales would plummet. Impact is essential. Brilliant creative copy and wonderful graphic design can get you noticed, but will it be read? A shocking headline may be read, but will it be believed? Review your Persona Credibility Index at least once every three months to monitor whether your high-impact message is credible to your audience.

Mini Persona Profile: Enquiring Media

The National Enquirer is high impact. People in grocery-store lines read the headlines and indulge their urge to read about the 200-pound baby or the dog-faced boy. But do they believe? Most smile, browse, and some even buy. But they do not believe. *The National Enquirer* is currently trying to lure mainstream advertisers to its magazine. Distribution is high at 5.5 million readers, so why wouldn't advertisers want to spend money on a page? Most wouldn't consider the *Enquirer,* because their persona would become associated with such tabloid magazines. Until *The National Enquirer* becomes more credible, credible advertisers will avoid its pages.

28—Code of Reach

How do you reach everyone who could buy your product? Sometimes you can't or shouldn't. But in most industries, you have to reach thousands of members of your audience to secure a single sale. Reach is one of the most frustrating formulas in advertising. Media directors crunch numbers to show clients how many Gross Reach Points they'll achieve in their audience (the gross number of times your audience is reached). Interpreting the GRP calculation is usually one area in which marketing departments and entrepreneurs feel quite uncomfortable.

Once you know this number, you should ask the question: "What medium is best to reach my audience that number of times?" Don't be intimidated. Reach is a crucial cornerstone of your marketing efforts. The hard part is knowing how many times you should reach your audience. Once you have this number, developing a media plan is a numbers game anyone can play, as long as you have the patience.

29—Code of the Unexpected

Never do what your customers and competitors expect. Adopt military strategies and surprise your enemy. Do the unexpected— always making sure the unexpected contains your core message. Some ventures go too far in the quest for the unexpected, and their message becomes meaningless. At this point, your Persona Credibility Index becomes important. You can be totally unexpected only if you have a credible product. Most products can benefit from a small dose of the unexpected, especially if they have many competitors.

Mini Persona Profile: Miller Neon

Unexpected does not mean irrelevant. Miller Beer proved this with a striking television campaign that showed a giant neon cowboy come to life, stepping down from the side of a Las Vegas casino into the street to pursue a huge, frosty Miller Genuine Draft on the side of a delivery truck. Completed with realistic animation, the sudden movement of the neon sign is entirely unexpected. Beer is beer. The benefits are largely the same for all competitors. But Miller blew away the competition by taking an unexpected turn in its advertising, which set it apart from the dozens of competitors who relied on monotonous lifestyle ads. It worked. At the time of the campaign, Genuine Draft was the only nonlight premium enjoying share growth.

30—Code of the Turnaround

There are many ways to engineer a turnaround. If you have a failing venture or you're in a stagnant segment, you can use many of the Persona Codes to reengineer your venture. If your venture is failing, you must commit to either complete reengineering—using the Codes of Invention, Knowledge, Ownership, Rationales, Impact, and Reach—or you must kill the venture. A slow death is painful for everyone: staff, clients, and yourself. The first step to implementing a turnaround is to get past the "kill the venture" option. This is unfair to all participants in your venture. The best solution is to re-engineer your persona. Like everything else, this process starts with a Persona Inventory.

31—Code of War

If you know about military strategy, you know that marketing is war. Strategies such as ambush, taking the high ground, and espionage are powerful in business. If you think of your venture as an army—with you as the general, your staff as your soldiers, and your competition as the enemy—you will start to think strategically. War has a way of energizing and motivating. The great leaders don't battle for survival. They develop strategies, innovations, and opportunities based on the tested techniques of humankind's most terrible profession: that of the soldier. This is why many business executives study the millennia-old wisdom of Sun Tzu in *The Art of War*. "Taking the high ground" becomes analogous to finding an advantage over your competitor. "Ambush when they do not expect" calls to mind the Persona Code of the Unexpected. "Never attack a larger force" means there is no value in marketing against the leader—only in finding a niche or an opportunity. The strategies of warfare can all be applied in the marketing arena.

32—Code of Direction

Never change your direction. You do so at risk of your entire investment. Most of the recent corporate failures resulted when companies tried to change direction. Keep tightly focused on your *singular* purpose. This does not mean you should be totally inflexible and unresponsive to competitors, audiences, and the economy. Your main goals and your mission must be inflexible; however, your path to achievement can take minor detours to avoid hazards. Nevertheless, the major direction should not change. Every direction change reduces your Image Equity to almost zero.

33—Code of Campaigns

Campaigns have equity value and should be considered over any single marketing efforts. Each element of any campaign must contribute to a single Persona development. Even after you have established "top of mind" in your audience, stay with your successful campaigns. Avoid orphan ads that do not contribute to your Persona Plan. Consistent ad campaigns—regardless of budget—have many times the power of individual ads, though they may offer various benefits that have the same reach. The audience only wants to know your main benefit. You hurt your venture by trying to tell them everything.

34—Code of Strategy
Never leave anything to chance. Orchestrate every element of your business and life—from lunch reservations to media placements. Your most valuable strategic weapons are your Persona Plan, your Marketing Plan, and your Business Plan. Strategy can only come out of accurate research. Don't leave your venture to chance. You can engineer your success through research, strategy, and consistency.

35—Code of Humanity
Although the persona must be rigid to build equity, it is valuable to occasionally personalize your iron Image requirements with apparent rule-breaking. Being a human being to your clients is important. The key to succeeding with this Code is to write your "inconsistency" strategy into your Persona Plan. Instruct your staff to send handwritten notes once in a while to remind customers you are human beings. As a break from your rigid campaigning, sponsor a Daily Bread Food Bank by volunteering your entire office and doing a little PR. Recognize that these are minor planned variances. Don't suddenly abandon a successful image just because you want to appear more human. Your persona is engineered through research, not instinct, but some human characteristics round out your persona nicely.

36—Code of Dreams
Your persona starts with your dreams! Your dreams become objectives. Continue to dream long after you begin living your persona, and long after your persona has a life of its own. Eventually, dreams become realities—if you want them badly enough!

37—Code of Testimonials
Credibility is mission one, and testimonials are a fast way to achieve this mission. Make it your first duty to ask for testimonials from anyone who is happy with you, and use them at every opportunity. Testimonials can be valuable in marketing and are almost indispensable to any service provider. Almost any prospect will ask for

references when hiring a professional consultant or service provider. The best way to cultivate top references is to ask for them. Make sure that every satisfied customer writes you a letter. Some companies buy their endorsements by advertising with high-profile experts or celebrities. Generally, experts have more credibility and celebrities have more impact. Choose your own method based on your Persona Credibility Index rating.

38—Code of Truth

Lifestyle studies unanimously indicate that a swelling percentage of consumers do not trust advertising. This is the same majority that believes that politicians are all dishonest. The greed of the 1980s has given way to the cynicism of the 1990s. The only weapon effective enough to address this lack of trust is truth. If you can't prove it, don't say it. Even Nike is running testimonial ads to prove its claims. Money-back guarantees are the minimum requirement of retailing in these cynical times. Build your persona on a foundation of provable truths.

39—Code of the ASS

Never assume anything. Even small assumptions trap you. Nothing destroys hard-built persona faster than misunderstandings. Do extensive research. Inventory everything. Get agreements in writing. Verbal contracts that are reliant on your memory are suicidal in business.

Mini Persona Profile: Assuming Success

The leader is always vulnerable. This is because the leader often believes his position is invulnerable. Fast-food restaurants have allowed assumptions of security to jeopardize their market shares. Both Burger King and Kentucky Fried Chicken experienced market share drops valued at over $2 billion each. Likewise, Dairy Queen and Domino's experienced market-share drops of hundreds of millions. This problem is symptomatic of industry's assumption that positions are invulnerable. Burger King will always be number two to McDonald's, right? And KFC will always be more popular than Little Caesar's. These are the type of assumptions that lead to sloppy Persona marketing. Burger King and KFC have experimented regularly with different advertising styles—to the detriment of their positions. They assumed their equity was so secure that they couldn't lose by trying different personas. Yet these assumptions cost them billions.

40—Code of Gossip

Don't gossip! Don't allow your staff to do it. Dismiss gossipers from your company. Eliminate gossipers from your social circles. Gossip is unreliable and damages persona, morale, and relationships. Never bad-mouth your competition, suppliers, or clients.

41—Code of Fashion

Create trends—don't follow them. By the time you follow a trend, you are destined for number five spot. To be number one, you must create a trend. Avoid simple fads that don't last. A trend has equity. And if you created it, you own it. Make it fashionable for others to be like you.

42—Code of Acting

Most of the great actors and stars built great personas. John Wayne is John Wayne. No matter what movie he starred in, he was John Wayne, the American icon. John Wayne was not his name, but who cares? Is this a fraud? Our answer is no. John Wayne's marketers simply built his persona based on his true character.

All businesses can learn from actors. The techniques of acting and star-building are valuable to persona development. Controlling exterior action, expression, and tone to achieve a specific audience response is the goal of both great actors and great personas. Invest in acting classes and sales training for your publicly visible staff.

43—Code of The Environment

One trend is here to stay. Ventures that ignore the movement to preserve our resources and environment do so at their peril. Regardless of your personal beliefs, your customized persona must include a visible commitment to environmental responsibility. Use recycled paper. Reduce or eliminate waste and pollution. If you build these efforts into your persona, your audience will reward you. You will feel better about your company and improve morale. Environmental services were estimated as a $100 billion industry in 1994, a clear indication that your audience, regardless of your industry, demands environmental responsibility.

44—Code of Equity

Everything you do, say, and present can add to or take away from your Image-Equity. From the way you train your staff to answer the phone to the specifics of your advertising campaign, you must develop strategies that build. Negative image destroys hard-earned equity. No element of image is insignificant when you're building your equity. One bad word from one unhappy client can destroy a marketing effort. One hungover employee answering the phone can jeopardize a sale. One poorly considered ad can destroy a company's hard-earned position. This is why we have built Persona around eighty-eight specific codes of conduct. All of these codes are important to your Image-Equity.

45—Code of Calls

Never stop calling for new business. Through telephone calls, advertising, and personal contact you should never let people forget you. Even if you are so successful that you can take on no new work, don't ease up on prospecting. If you stop marketing when you get to the top, you will find your competitors scrambling to fill the void. Your future is never guaranteed, so never rest on your laurels.

46—Code of Symbols

Symbols have power. From primitive times on, symbols have been respected, feared, loved, and given magical attributes. Many of these symbols are archetypes that are part of the collective consciousness. Your audience can respond very positively or very negatively to a symbol.

Company logos are only one type of symbol. As the marketplace becomes increasingly fragmented and the media more diverse, the audience needs a stable image of your venture. In this Age of Confusion, when it is so difficult to be noticed, a logo can grant you instant recall, credibility, and impact. A logo can also destroy your credibility. As with any important element of your persona, only the best should be hired to produce logos.

Unlike advertising campaigns and other elements of marketing, a logo will last for the lifetime of your venture. If it is poorly executed, you will lose goodwill. If it is creatively and strategically executed, you can gain credibility from the day you open your business. A logo is a symbol of your persona. Like any symbol, it must perfectly reflect the idea behind it. Some symbols, such as the Playboy bunny and the Nike swoosh, have an identity all their own. With so much equity, the ventures these symbols represent no longer even need to state their name. Spend as much time and money as it takes to develop a logo that strategically fulfills your Persona Plan. After your name, your logo is your most important Persona statement.

47—Code of Targeting

Generation X. The Ike Generation. Baby Boomers. These are just the generic groups marketers target. In an age when media is diversifying and advertisers no longer have an economical way to reach all of their audience, two things have happened: specialized advertisers can focus very specific messages at very specific groups; and consumer advertisers can't reach audiences economically. Because of the high costs of reaching audiences in today's multimedia environment, tightly focused targeting is a necessity.

Who is the audience? What age? What sex? What sexual preference? What profession? What political ties? What social values? How many children do they have and of what age? Finding out the answers to questions like these is mandatory to your success. If you don't take the trouble to research everything there is to know about your audience, you'll never know whom to reach. If you don't know who to reach you'll end up spending too much to market your venture. Very few companies can afford mass marketing. Selective marketing requires targeting.

48—Code of Quality

According to Persona, quality is job two. Job one is letting people know you have quality. You can never own the word quality in your prospect's mind, because it's too general and everyone claims it. Even though it is worthless to advertise that you have quality—since it's demanded of every product—you must always maintain a higher quality standard than your competition. Long-term success depends on the quality of your offering. Quality is the one area left in marketing that can grow sales by word-of-mouth. The days of word-of-mouth advertising is generally gone in the complex markets of today; however, extraordinary quality—that reaches far beyond the norm—can still result in major sales gains through reputation.

Mini Persona Profile: Starbucks' Quality

It is a small luxury, but a luxury almost anyone can afford: a decent cup of coffee. Starbucks Coffee Corp. is the leader in the billion-dollar coffee industry. In the beginning, Starbucks marketed by offering free samples. The word got around. Later, when marketing became more traditional, the company focused on its quality offering, with ads that showed the source of its original reputation—the finest ingredients. This quality-first strategy grew Starbucks to sales in 1993 of $163.5 million.

49—Code of Energy

All of your energy should be committed to only one objective. Never divide your forces. (This is a standard tactic of war.) Most great battles (such as D day) are won with a single, massive, irresistible force that is undivided and full of energy. When you attack, pick only one target and go in with all you've got. Momentum of energy can be achieved through dedication to only one goal. Your staff will be motivated by the clarity of your mission. Your customers will trust you because of your simplicity. Your prospects will absorb your message because it is easy. Your energy will translate into revenues. And it will make you strong.

50—Code of Slogans

There are three points to the persona identity triangle: name, logo, and slogan. All companies must invest in a slogan that positions them to their audience. The slogan must be credible, easy to remember, unique, and short. These will become the words you apply exclusively to your venture. You will have to write the entire positioning statement—your unique difference—in five words or less. You will discover your slogan as you develop your Persona Inventory. Discovering all your assets and liabilities gives you the building blocks for developing a powerful slogan.

A slogan, like a logo and name, can damage your venture as much as help it. Therefore, it's too important to develop haphazardly. Your slogan will define your persona and must be carefully worded. You will not change your slogan for many years, and when you do, you'll evolve it. So make sure it appeals first to the target audience—or they won't buy—and second to you—because you'll have to live with it for years.

Mini Persona Profile: It's All in the Words

Most successful enterprises follow the Persona Code of Slogans. For example, the top three rental car companies—Hertz, Enterprise and Avis—were very close in 1994 sales with $2.1 billion, $1.85 billion, and $1.7 billion respectively. They have one important marketing element in common: all three have slogans that are short, easy to remember, and differentiating. Hertz, as the leader, merely uses the slogan "Hertz exactly." Second-place Enterprise states the way in which it is different: "We'll pick you up." Avis follows Persona Code 26 by emphasizing its weakness as a strength: "We try harder." Budget, in fourth place, plays on its main strength and its name: "The smart money is on Budget." All are successful and proven slogans. They state the unique benefit of each venture. They're short. And they help these companies earn billions each.

51—Code of Being Easy

Make everything easy for your prospect: offer easy-to-remember words and names, easy-to-remember toll-free phone numbers, easy-to-find offices, easy-to-access staff and service. Every aspect of your endeavor that is even slightly difficult gives your audience an opportunity to shop elsewhere.

52—Code of Advertising

Advertising is everything you do that your audience sees. Everything from the way you dress to your ad campaign must be in harmony with your one true message and persona. Don't worry about creating clever ads. Simplicity sells better. In the nineties, simple short copy consistently has tested more effectively than complicated or clever ads.

Discover your unique difference, and your ads will almost write themselves. Don't create your own ads unless you have expertise in this area. Advertising requires a fine balance of target audience needs and wants, benefit and feature offerings, and credibility and impact. A poorly crafted ad can make an otherwise credible company appear untrustworthy. An untalented spot featuring the founder of your company can make your otherwise brilliant company seem unsuccessful. A too-clever ad written by your marketing person may offend or even be ridiculed. Although advertising has less effect on your equity than a logo or slogan, it has a cumulative effect. Make too many mistakes, change directions too many times, or offend too many people, and you will not be taken seriously.

53—Code of Invention

To succeed, you must invent something. Invent a new product or service, find a new marketing niche for an existing product or service, or discover a new way of servicing an existing niche. Inventing a product gives you assured success, if the demand can be created. Inventing a new market niche for an existing product is the only way to succeed when there is entrenched competition. Inventing a new way of servicing an existing niche is the most common strategy for entry players, and it's also the weakest.

Sometimes the "invention" is just a way of differentiating your product from virtually identical products. Fruitopia, a heavily advertised new product from Coca-Cola, is an example. Other times the process of Persona Inventory can show you your real weaknesses and strengths and help you modify your existing offering so it becomes totally unique. The recent introduction of a perfume for babies, Le Petit Guerlain, is an example. And occasionally you can come up with something totally new for your market. Any of these strategies can work, provided you make your offering visible to your audience.

54—Code of Selling

Every person is a salesperson first. Even the CEOs of the largest companies are salespeople. Whether you are pitching to the board of directors or selling directly to your audience, you are a salesperson. Learn to sell like the best salesperson, no matter what your career choice or business. Take sales training courses or read sales motivational books and learn the steps of selling: prospecting, cold calling, qualification, handling objections, and closing. These are valuable techniques that would benefit a receptionist as much as a president. Sales techniques can teach you a lot about how to market your product. Salespeople often make good ad writers for this reason.

55—Code of Speculation

Speculation in any business damages persona. Any time you offer what you are selling free, you lose the perception of value. If you give away what you sell—in the hope people will buy it if they really like it—you have not understood selling. If you do not understand selling, you must perish. Any client who demands speculative presentations is not worth having. He will inevitably pay less (if he pays at all) and take advantage of you and all your competitors. If a client does not understand why asking you to work speculatively is wrong, he cannot be trusted.

56—Code of Maturity

One of the most important criteria for judging credibility is maturity. If you operate an established venture, you have a great deal of mature equity compared to a start-up. You may want to change your positioning or strategy after a Persona Inventory, but your company's years in business can still lend credibility to your new direction. You can gain extraordinary marketing mileage out of a well-established history. For example, IBM is undergoing major management, developmental, and marketing changes, but it will never destroy its hard-earned name recognition by creating an apparent revolution. The company is evolving its Persona. Start-up companies should avoid entirely the issue of age in their marketing. The best launch is nonlaunch. Don't announce grand openings, new products, or revolutionary services. They have no credibility. People don't want to be the first to try something new (with the exception of a very small percentage of techno-junkies, who enjoy buying into the latest idea). Even if your product or service is revolutionary, avoid radical marketing statements.

57—Code of Loyalty

Building relationships is at the heart of long-term marketing. A large percentage of ventures now spend large portions of their marketing budgets on building loyalty. This is because it is less costly to offer rewards for loyalty than it is to generate a replacement customer if the competition lures a regular away. Reward your clients with a personally written letter from the CEO, a reward points program, a follow-up phone call, a no-questions-asked merchandise replacement policy—these are all powerful ways of cultivating loyalty.

Mini Persona Profile: Rewarding Points

American Airline's Advantage frequent-flyer program has 23 million members. These members fly more than 25,000 miles per year. The rewards of loyalty often cost the client being rewarded, in terms of increased fares. The cost of the marketing program at American keeps the airline uncompetitive on fares with discount carriers like Southwest Airlines. Yet it maintains its position as the first choice of business travelers through its rewards policy and its service. Similarly, American Express rewards keep people using a credit card that retailers would rather not accept. A number of department stores offer loyalty points to keep people out of discount superstores. These days, loyalty programs are no longer the exception; they are becoming the rule.

58—Code of Networking

Networking outside of your trade is always important. Networking inside your trade is dangerous and leaves you exposed. Always network only with prospects—never with your competitors. Join the trade associations of your prospects. Only join the trade associations of your trade if it gives you credibility or is educational. Otherwise you risk revealing to your competitors your strengths and weaknesses.

59—Code of Expert

Become an expert. You can make yourself an expert in two ways: learn everything that you can about your field and work with the knowledge so intensely that it becomes second nature, or create your own specialty in which you are the only acknowledged expert. Of course, creating a niche requires a vast knowledge of the category to begin with, and it must be something your audience is interested in. There is tremendous credibility in being able to claim expert status in a certain field. Promote your expertise at every opportunity.

Mini Persona Profile: The Asian Expert

Cathay Pacific, once considered a British airline, has re-Personified itself as the world's Asian airline. This is a calculated Persona move. Cathay can never be the acknowledged expert in the overall airline industry. Worldwide it is one of the five most profitable airlines. Now, however, it is the number one "Asian international airline." A new logo solidifies the new persona—a logo stylized to look like Asian calligraphy. Cathay's new advertising campaigns use brushstroke-style type rendering. The airline's campaign solidifies its new persona: "With over 650 flights per week to and from Hong Kong, no one gives you more strength than Cathay Pacific, the heart of Asia."

60—Code of Regularity

Unwavering, stubborn dedication to one direction is crucial. You must make a splash to be noticed (see Code 11, Code of the Race) and then you must never change direction or focus. If you change strategy, you must begin with a new Persona Plan and forfeit all the equity you have built. You should only undertake this strategy if there is a powerful rationale for doing so—a Persona Plan that demands a radical change because of weaknesses shown in the Inventory.

61—Code of Talent

Your persona should be built on a foundation of genuine skills and assets. In building your persona, choose your most marketable talents, find a viable audience, and Image-Market your talents at every opportunity. Discovery of your unique talents should not happen by accident. If you do not wish to undertake a Persona Inventory, informally or formally poll your clients, prospects, staff, and partners. Once you've discovered your unique talent, promote your differentiated image.

62—Code of Change

Never change what works. Most of the spectacular failures in big business were caused by unnecessary changes in image where none was warranted. Some of the greatest successes are accomplished by companies and people who *never* change what works. Don't be afraid of the label *old-fashioned*; it also means reliable and valuable. Fix only what needs fixing. Eventually, you may have to update. This is an evolutionary change. For example, Chrysler updated the design of its best-selling minivans. Even though it was still the market leader, it saw aggressive competition and its own stale design as a future handicap. Proactively, Chrysler evolved the design. It did not jeopardize what works, because it did not claim to be "replacing" it. Such revolutions should be reserved for disaster relief.

63—Code of Courtesy

Never get tired of saying thank you. Say it so often that you feel embarrassed to say it anymore. Get in the powerful habit of thanking people in writing. Send out at least one thank-you card every day for life. Always say thank you twice as often as anyone else. It is the most powerful phrase in any language. People remember your courtesy. Every one of your clients deserves at least twelve thank-you's every year. Say thank you in your advertising as well. Friendly service is promoted by companies as diverse as Mobil and your neighborhood hardware store. It may not be a unique message, but courtesy is a mandatory element of any persona.

64—Code of Pause

When you do not know something, never admit it. Find a reason for a pause or break, or say something like "That's too important to answer lightly. I'd like to analyze the problem before I give an answer." But never answer that you do not know. And never answer incorrectly. Pause, think, analyze, research—then give the correct answer. You will never be respected for your speedy answers. You will be respected for your thoughtfulness and precision.

65—Code of Dress

Even though we are moving into the "decade of substance," appearances still count. First impressions are formed from the way you dress, the appearance of your office and the way you speak, and the style of your logo and advertising. These priorities will never change. Ultimately, your audience is concerned only with your substance. But to capture its attention and to gain credibility you must dress to fit your persona—down to the finest detail. Your dress code is the walking advertisement for your persona. Clothes and manners do influence decisions.

Mini Persona Profile: The Casual Trio

In mid-October of 1994, Steven Spielberg, Jeffrey Katzenberg, and David Geffen announced the formation of a new film and record company, Dreamworks SKG. They appeared on television and in magazines wearing casual clothes with unbuttoned collars and no jackets. Is this the persona of a new company potentially worth billions? The casual persona is every bit as relevant as the formal persona. Sega executives would do well to appear young and dress grunge. IBM recently renounced its long-standing suit dress code. You dress to fulfill your persona. But your persona should be focused on what appeals to your target audience.

66—Code of Strength

Attack only from a position of strength. Do everything possible to make certain the outcome will be in your favor: dress correctly, research your prospect, show only your best accomplishments, and only meet when you are in your best form. Good military commanders do not attack until they *know* they can win.

Does this contradict our earlier statement that "the underdog usually wins"? Not at all. The underdog, because of the weaker position, will innovate. These innovations become strengths that in turn become weapons in the marketing war. If you are the small player in your industry you must work harder. Sometimes, this means you simply have to say, "We're number two, so we try harder," and sometimes it is more involved, and you may have to improve your product or service to make it better than that of the competition. Whatever strategy you employ, do not begin your marketing attack until you have the strength to win. If you only have 10 percent of the budget of your competitor, perhaps you should target a narrower audience that you can capture. If you can't open enough stores to compete with your rival's 1,000 shops, perhaps you should franchise. There is always an innovative solution that can put you in a position of strength.

67—Code of Competence

Only speak or write what you *know* to be true. If you are only 90 percent certain, do not speak. If you are guessing, speak only if you like losing. Speak and write only in situations in which you are competent. Likewise, let others speak in their areas of competence. And speak infrequently. Silence is power.

68—Code of Contrasts

Never copy anyone else's success. This does not mean you should stop studying the wisdom of the successful. Read case studies, study, admire, envy, and learn—but don't copy. If you copy something, you must compete with that something. If you compete with the already successful, you will likely fail. You must make your own route to success, learning the lessons of others, but charting your own way. If, however, you are content to be number two, aware that you will never be number one, your strategy must become one of admitting you are in second place. In this case, second place can be its own niche.

Mini Persona Profile: Say "Bye" to Neon

The Code of Contrasts is most obvious when you make competitive comparisons. Generally, this is unwise, unless you are reflecting positively on the differences and avoiding negative criticisms of the competition. This is exactly the strategy Pontiac is following with the Sunfire. The launch campaign proclaims "Say Bye to Neon. A well-made car for under $8500." This is a fun play on Chrysler's brilliant "Say Hi to Neon" campaign which targets college students. In this case, Pontiac does not criticize the competition. It merely states its selling hook: "A well-made car for under $8500."

69—Code of Foreshadowing

One of the most powerful techniques in building a persona—and in selling any of your ideas—is foreshadowing. Never go in cold. Always hint at how expensive you might be, and tease your audience every chance you can with your strengths. If you know the reaction to your message will be negative, prepare the audience. If you already know all the objections a prospective client is going to hit you with, hit him first by answering the objections in your sales pitch or advertisement. Foreshadow your price, deadlines, delivery problems—anything which could cause future grief. You cannot afford client ill will. You project a negative image if you are constantly making excuses. You project a positive image if you prepare your client for the worst in advance.

70—Code of Reliability

Never cancel, postpone, or apologize. Apologies are signals from people who never fulfill their commitments. Leaders always fulfill *every* commitment. Set deadlines and appointments for everything you do—even family outings—then keep each one. Punish yourself severely when you miss even an unimportant appointment or break a promise. Your persona cannot survive a reputation for unreliability.

71—Code of Familiarity

Avoid familiarity in any professional relationship. Friendship destroys business relationships. Formality solidifies them. Familiarity leads to a damaging and rapid downward spiral in credibility and reputation. You become the flawed friend instead of the hero. Appear friendly, but do not be a friend to your clients. By all means feel good about your audience, like them, even love them if you wish, but *never* confide in them.

72—Code of the Bribe

Don't buy your business through direct incentives except as a last resort. Promotions in marketing do nothing but damage your persona. Even discounters suffer equity loss when they offer promotions; giving further discounts on the discounts implies they were not expensive to begin with. The exception to the rule occurs when pure consumer products are involved that cannot be easily differentiated. Promotions are a poor strategy in marketing because the competition

usually responds in kind. Eventually, the discounted price becomes the normal price. This leads to further rounds of discounting until the lowest margin threshold is reached.

Some marketers excuse this clumsy method of marketing by saying that giving the discount is less expensive than building an image or persona. This may be true, but it leads to a path of diminishing returns. Eventually, you'll be left with no image, because you didn't invest in your persona, just a product with a very small margin. Mature brands often begin offering aggressive promotions as their shares decline. Again, this is a strategic error. Ten years of equity in the brand can be blown away with two years of promotions. The correct approach to this problem is to revitalize the persona. Top of Mind can achieve what promotions and bribes cannot—long-term growth.

73—Code of Power

Power comes directly from your profile. Be noticed everywhere. Engineer invitations to important events. Volunteer for *high profile* and important organizations. If you have time, serve on all the advisory committees that will have you. Try for chairperson titles of important government committees or charities. Be seen anywhere your audience might see you. From your profile—and ultimately your persona—will flow your power.

Cultivate your power. Donate money to publicized causes. Chair panel discussions on your local trade association's lunch seminars. Keep in touch with your trade magazines and regional press through regular press releases that trumpet your accomplishments. Offer your services as an expert when a journalist needs an opinion. Profile is power.

Monopoly can give you the highest level of power. The next best strategy is to make sure you are known to be the inventor of your niche. Microsoft's Bill Gates is one of the most powerful men in America, not because he is the richest but because his company's software is on practically every PC in the world.

74—Code of Damage Control

If you cannot avoid a major disaster that affects your audience, learn the principles of public relations. While public relations is not a worthwhile expenditure in marketing for general Imaging or marketing, it becomes indispensable if you are in a crisis situation. Avoid the rumor mill by being the one who brings the bad news—but *only* if you know someone will find out. Using PR techniques—or hiring a qualified crisis public relations agency—is the best way to handle public damage control. Internal disasters that affect client work—but not your end result to the client—should never be revealed (see Code 26, Code of Weakness).

75—Code of Detail

Do not paint in broad strokes. Your Persona Plan for yourself—and any plans for your audience—must be drawn in the finest detail. One rude employee, a customer left on hold, a forgotten call-back or a late appointment—these are the small brushstrokes that kill deals and promotions.

76—Code of Clairvoyance

Know your future. Never guess at outcomes. If you can't absolutely say for certain what an outcome will be, you have not done enough planning, research, and rehearsal. Either learn to predict the future accurately, or create the future you want.

77—Code of Drilling

Drill and practice for power. Practice your techniques on your relatives. Show your persona elements—logo, slogan, name, and so on—to all of your associates in an informal focus session. Pitch to the mirror. Drill and redrill your staff until they are perfect. Learn the valuable lessons of the army—which has a splendid program for training raw civilians in only weeks. Do the same with yourself and your staff. Do not rest until you achieve perfection. As in the case of a soldier, your life may depend on it.

78—Code of Technology

Make technology your ally and never your enemy. Keep up to date with the latest computers, phone systems, and information highway technology. Technology is changing the world radically on an almost yearly basis, so keep up or risk losing what you have built. Build technology into your persona and your product. Keep up to date on the latest media, especially interactive computer media, to make sure your venture is exposed there in the most efficient way.

Mini Persona Profile: Cadillac Goes Digital

Cadillac is driving "the information highway" with its computer disk interactive marketing campaign. It is also advertising on the on-line services Prodigy and CompuServe. The strategy behind the aggressive embracing of technology is Image. Cadillac, the upper-middle-class older gentleman's car, is targeting the highly educated, affluent baby boomers. These buyers typically buy import luxury autos, but they can be swayed by progressive technology. The use of technology to convince prospects that Cadillac is progressive is one brilliant example of Persona Planning.

79—Code of Doctors

Rely on the very best image doctors and consultants. Any skill that you do not possess at the highest levels, you must acquire. It is less expensive to acquire specialized expertise through consultants than through internal development. Hire only the best ad agencies, programmers, marketing consultants, accountants, doctors, and lawyers. You deserve the best advice possible—and it is almost always worth the price. The Persona Planning Process will allow you to save considerable time and money through self-help research and analysis. Execution of your plans, for areas outside of your normal expertise, are best handled by specialists.

80—Code of Hype

Hype is a beautiful word. Hype must be no more and no less than your truth. The energy of hype forces everyone to become aware of the truth. Hype all of your truths at every opportunity. Our definition of hype does not allow you to exaggerate the facts, but it does allow you to demonstrate your facts in the most dramatic and emphatic way possible. The level of hype you can safely use will depend on your Persona Credibility Index. A low index will allow for maximum hype and vice versa. Make people accept that you are number one in your niche. Let everyone know you are the best. Never tire of hype.

81—Code of Price

Position price as part of your detailed Persona Plan. The value of your offer is fundamental to your success. The value of an offering is the most tangible measure of your Image-Equity. The higher your image value, the higher the price. The lower your image value, the less influence you have over the price. This can be the most important element of your Persona Plan. Price is a major component of image. Lower price—regardless of real value—equals lower image.

Sometimes the mere act of tagging a ridiculously high price on to a product makes it seem more desirable—but only for prestige products that appeal to middle- to upper-class audiences. Giving a small discount on a profitable brand can change consumer perceptions equally, permanently damaging Image-Equity. Don't play with prices without a good deal of careful audience-response research. Test in small samples before committing to a full price change. Even service businesses can test pricing by quoting different prices to gauge response.

Price is the one aspect of image that must be carefully monitored. Sales are a good benchmark against which to set prices, as are competitor sales.

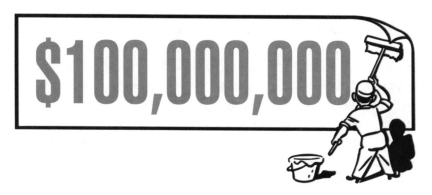

82—Code of Mistakes

Everyone makes them—but every mistake damages the persona you have built. Learn the strategy for making almost no mistakes. Build a foolproof level of protection into your Persona Plan. Then, when a rare mistake happens, make sure *no one* knows about it. Divorce yourself completely from associates and employees who make many mistakes. Divorce yourself completely from products that have no potential. Mistakes are always remembered. Perfection rarely is— unless you promote it.

83—Code of Eagerness

You should always be hungry and eager—but you must never appear to beg. The desperate are never taken seriously. The best strategy for obtaining the seemingly unobtainable is to appear not to care. This is not the same as being rude or showing no interest. A carefully crafted, very calm routine will assure your prospects that you can handle their demands. An overly eager and energetic pitch can seem pathetic. Even when you lose a deal—and you will—smile, say thank you, and act as if it didn't make any difference to your bottom line. Send the lost client a polite thank-you card that just says, "Enjoyed meeting. See you next time."

84—Code of Twos

Then there were two. There can never be more than one competitor— two in a niche. The third, fourth, and fifth—no matter how temporarily successful they might be—must eventually start down the road of diminishing returns. Number two almost always has half the business of number one. Some large categories can accommodate up to ten competitors, but only if each carves out a specific niche. For example, in rental cars you have three companies that specialize in lower pricing, two that pick you up, and four that claim excellent service. Even with this differentiation, over the long haul several of these competitors will either fail or change. No industry has ever been able to support more than three main competitors in a major segment for longer than seven years. Don't waste your valuable resources on a losing proposition. Evolve your product away from the crowded mainstream into a category all your own. Then, later, when a second competitor joins you, you will be the number one.

Mini Persona Profile: Twin Soft Drinks

There are dozens of soft drinks, aren't there? Yes. But there are only two colas: number one Coke and number two Pepsi. Pepsi is proud of its number two spot. Its taste-test campaign builds momentum on its underdog position. What about Dr. Pepper? Dr. Pepper is alone, filling a unique niche. Diet Coke and Diet Pepsi fight it out in another head-to-head battle. Sprite and 7UP battle for the Uncola title. Each of these master marketing companies realized that it could not survive in a field of ten. Officially they are ranked in order of market share as follows: Coke Classic, Pepsi, Diet Coke, Dr. Pepper, Diet Pepsi, Mountain Dew, Sprite, 7UP, Caffeine-Free Diet Coke, Caffeine-Free Pepsi. But these individual sodas do not truly compete in the same markets. The Coke drinker is not the same customer as the 7 UP drinker. Occasionally people will dabble across categories, but most consumers consistently stay with one of the twin categories: Colas from number one Coke and number two Pepsi; Uncolas from number one Sprite and number two 7UP; Diet colas from number one Diet Coke and number two Diet Pepsi. The Code of Twos applies ultimately to any category. Those categories with more than two main contenders are supporting only temporary situations, eventually to stabilize into a twin market.

85—Code of the Vigilante

Never depend on outside forces to bring you "justice" or your "due." The truth is that no one owes you anything. You will only achieve by becoming the vigilante of your cause. Do not file complaints—make your own justice. Do not pout—move forward aggressively. Vigilantes never wait for someone else. If the rest of the world cannot keep up with your "Batman" image, you have succeeded.

86—Code of the Last Place

You're the last in. You're in last place. What do you do? Although the Code of Twos states that you cannot survive long in last place (unless last place is second place), there are a number of strategies you can employ. You can create your own niche. You can try harder and let everyone know it. If you choose to "try harder" in anything below second place, however, you must have a long-term strategy in place to evolve your offering into a new niche. Your years will be numbered if you are satisfied with number three, four, five, or six. Alternatively you can employ a ruthless strategy to unseat the number two player. Unless this player makes a major mistake, though, success in this ball game is statistically unlikely. Don't be satisfied with being that "other" gadget. Don't be an also-ran.

Mini Persona Profile: The Subversive Persona

If you can't change your product or service and you are not terrified by our statement that last-place contenders never survive, you can differentiate your venture through Persona Positioning. Your product may be the same, but what you choose to say about it is different. It is this strategy that has led to some of the wackier image campaigns. RC Cola, for instance, broadcasts zany ads that show consumers actually being reeled in by Pepsi and Coke fishermen. The final shot shows these hapless consumers hanging upside down like trophies. Then you hear the overdubbed line, "Hey, you don't have to swallow that." This is violent, subversive, and radical advertising, just what you need when you are last place. In essence, RC is carving out a culture niche, setting itself apart from the big colas. Again, Pepsi and Coke are left alone in their categories. But RC Cola has created its own Persona niche.

87—Code of the Ethics

Ethics is crucial to building the credibility of any persona. Write an ethical code, let everyone know your high standards, and then live it! A mission statement for your personal life and business, coupled with a written ethical code, are mandatory for success. Once it's published, never vary from it. And make it live up to high standards. If your persona ethical code is toothless, it will have no benefit. Make your code a crusade, and force others to live up to it.

88—Code of the Pride

No matter how successful you are, the day you become arrogant is the day you will fall. Pride in your achievements should be cultivated— but with grace. Everyone should know about your success—but never through your arrogance. Never alter your successful persona because you have become number one. The Jade Emperor must always fall—so be content to be a kind king.

PART FIVE

A PERSONA
HOW-TO

▼

"You don't stand a tinker's chance of producing successful advertising unless you start by doing your homework. I have always found this tedious, but there is no substitute for it...study the product. The more you know about it, the more likely you are to come up with a big idea for selling it."
David Ogilvy

Ogilvy On Advertising

Going It On
Your Own

▼

*"The questions which one asks oneself begin,
at last, to illuminate the world...."*
James Baldwin

Nobody Knows My Name

There is nothing complicated or difficult about developing a Persona Plan. It is not expensive or complex. There are three important steps:

★ Understand why the Persona Principle works and the basic underlying principles.
★ Conduct a full Persona Inventory of your current situation.
★ Develop a Persona Plan that fulfills your objectives in order of priorities.

Step 1
Learn the Factors and Codes
Begin by fully understanding the Persona Factors and Persona Codes. Reread the case studies. Think of other businesses you know that have succeeded because of their personas: chances are you can think of many.

Step 2
Inventory Your Persona Assets and Liabilities
Begin to list all the positives and negatives about your current venture. What works? What doesn't? What appeals to your audience? What doesn't? Don't stop to figure out how to solve your problems. Just get them all down first.

Step 3
Develop an Objectives-oriented Plan
Using the list of what works and what doesn't as your Persona Inventory, develop a comprehensive, step-by-step Persona Plan. The Persona Planning Process is easy. You have already identified the liabilities to your image in the previous step. Now write a solution to each of these problems, and set a priority for its execution.

In the execution of your Persona Plan, review your Persona Credibility Index and your Persona Compromise Quotient. By now you should have completed these important exercises. If you have not already done so, return to the chapters on the Credibility Factor and the No-Compromise Factor to determine your PCI and PCQ.

These ratings should guide you in the execution of your Persona Plan. If you are credible to your audience, create a moderate persona to prevent a loss of credibility. If you are incredible to your audience, create a conservative persona to build your credibility. If you have a tendency to compromise, set hard rules for execution that cannot be broken, then enforce them with ruthless zeal. If you never compromise, be prepared to build on the success of your Persona Plan.

Your Own Persona Planning Technique

Persona is a system that is proven to work if executed accurately. You have seen samples of this system in the mathematical structure of the Persona Credibility Index. It works because it sets an indexed number to all variables of different ventures. By creating a numerical standard, you can employ proven image-building techniques that can benefit any size or type of business. This technique is particularly useful if you do not intend to hire professionals to execute your ideas. If you have a tight budget or prefer self-help marketing, Persona is formulated for you.

It is not always necessary for you to invest the time to complete a formal Persona Plan. The *Persona Planning Guide* consists of 221 steps outlined in more than 200 pages and takes an average of six weeks to complete. The formal system requires a considerable investment of your time. You can achieve similar effects—although less consistent and measurable—by creating your own Persona Inventory and Persona Plan.

How To Create Your Own Persona Inventory

Be as formal or as informal as you like, but be complete. Write a question that reflects your venture's position with respect to each Persona Factor and Persona Code in this book. For example, your question for the Reality Factor might read:

"How true is our main claim to our target audience?"

You might then answer:

"Our main claim is that we are the longest-lasting stainless steel ball bearing in the marketplace. We

have proven this in several endurance tests, certified
by the federal government."

You should rate your answer as either a liability or an asset to your
persona. Because you're only conducting an informal inventory, this
will be a judgment call on your part. You simply decide whether your
answer to the question supports your image or damages it. If you are
in doubt, treat it as a liability.

Continue creating a question and answer for each factor and each
code, listing all pertinent facts and details in support of your answers.
Even if you are the only person who will read your Persona Inventory,
write the questions and answers so anybody, even a complete
stranger, could understand.

What you'll have at the end is ninety-six questions with ninety-six
answers—your own version of our Persona Inventory. You will not
have weighted your answers by importance or created a consistent
mathematical model that allows you to compare your venture to
 any other, but you'll have a starting point for your Persona Plan.
With this important information you will be able to set priorities
for execution.

How To Create Your Own Persona Plan

When you make your action list, remember that the Persona Factors are more important than the Persona Codes. The goal of the Persona Planning Process is to identify all your liabilities and then find ways to turn them into assets.

You can create your own Persona Plan or use the *Persona Planning Guide.* If you write your own system, your Persona Plan must identify four important areas:

★   Where you are now.
★   Where you need to be.
★   What tools and changes can help you get there.
★   What to do when.

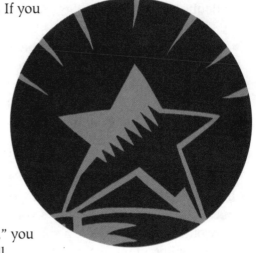

Where You Are Now

To identify "Where you are now," you can create a synopsis of your full inventory. Write a list, in order of importance, of all the liabilities identified in your Persona Inventory.

Where You Need to Be

The most difficult step in creating your own plan is to decide where you need to be. Essentially, this is goal-setting. Whatever type of plan you are creating—from business plan to Persona Plan—the objectives you set for yourself will determine your success. The important thing to remember about this step is that you must set realistic, achievable goals.

The easiest way to create a goal-oriented plan is to look at the smaller objectives first. Turn each liability into a goal. All goals are theoretically achievable. Even if you set a near-impossible goal, given enough money and time, plus the right strategy, it can be achieved. If you wish to be President of the United States, it's possible in theory. You might find the goal beyond your means, but given the necessary resources—lots of time, money, and support—you can achieve this goal, even if it takes a lifetime.

So much for theory. The reality of life for most of us is that our means dictate how far we can take our goals. I might have to settle for being mayor of my small town before I have enough credibility to run for governor. From governor, perhaps I can reach the presidency—after a lifetime of carefully planned personas.

You need to set achievable goals. If you don't have a lifetime of patience, or you don't have unlimited financing, settle for shorter-term goals. The short-term goals can lead to your lifetime objective. Set goals according to your means. Limit your ambitions to one-year goals at first, leaving your loftier goals for five- and ten-year plans.

One-year goals are easily stated. In the formal *Persona Planning Guide*, we use numbers and state goals in terms of a "lift." We can do this because every answer in the formal Persona Inventory has a numerical value. The lift is merely the difference between the Inventory value now and that which represents where you would like to be. While formal Persona Planning states lift as a number, the informal process usually describes it as a statement. You can state goals however you wish, as long as they are measurable. Goals stated in dollar terms are the most effective. Other goals should be stated as precisely as possible.

To illustrate, here's a typical informal Persona Inventory entry for the Credibility Factor:

> "Our audience does not believe that we are the best ball bearing manufacturer and tends to purchase ABC ball bearings, because they have been established for fifteen years. Our price is lower, but we are consistently in fourth place. Credibility is a major issue."

This particular liability must be addressed immediately, because it concerns a Persona Factor—the Credibility Factor. You can state objectives in any way that is helpful to you, as long as you know the importance of this step. You might state your objective regarding this problem this way:

> "We must consider credibility our most important objective. We can prove we have the best product but the message is not being received well. We will focus on our primary target audience of automotive manufacturers and communicate with them through conservative, credible messages. Our objective is to achieve 75 percent acceptance of our claim that we offer the most durable stainless steel ball bearing. This objective must be achieved within three years."

Once you've set your objective, you need only to decide how to attack the problem.

What Tools and Changes Can Help You Get There

The next planning step is to list all your options. Good or bad, expensive or not, list every possible tool and weapon you can think of. Brainstorm and write down all possible ways to turn your liability into an asset, putting a price and a time on each option. In our ball-bearing example, you could list these options:

★ We could stop using our claim "the most durable stainless steel ball bearing" and lower our price. This would overcome the credibility gap by eliminating the claim that is not credible. By claiming less, we will achieve our 75 percent acceptance goal quickly. Time: immediate effect. Cost: lost profits of at least 3¢ per ball bearing, potentially $450,000 per year on our current volume.

★ We could maintain our incredible-but-true claim and run an aggressive series of trade ads that prove our claim, showing the federal government regulations. Time: a minimum of two years, based on a carefully structured program of trade magazine ads that reach 75 percent of the audience at least twelve times. Cost: $375,000, based on monthly insertions in every major trade magazine for two years.

★ We could raise our prices. In conjunction with a high-end brochure, such an increase can reposition us as offering the better-quality product. Time: immediate decrease in sales, slower impact on positioning. Cost: projected drop in revenues of $300,000 through loss of existing clientele.

Once you've established your options, you must decide which one will work for you. Write an impact report. Decide what the effect of each option would be:

★ Lowering the standards of our quality claim will likely increase immediate unit sales but reduce long-term business by supporting the perception that our quality is inferior.

★ We cannot afford the expense of a major positioning campaign, even though it would likely work over the long term.

★ We would lose some clientele, but only the smaller operators. We could potentially gain large contracts, especially from government agencies.

You must then decide on your course of action. Sometimes the answer is obvious. In the above example, you might decide that lowering standards will not work and that you are not willing to invest in a major image campaign. You might decide to test the third option with a short-term price increase in a selected market. It is never recommended that you radically change the image you project to your entire market. Even with extensive research, to do so is a gamble, and at stake is the equity you have earned in your market. Play it safe and test your plan on a small segment first.

If you still can't decide on an option, go back to your Persona Inventory and research the background of the liability in more depth. Then brainstorm more options. If you cannot determine satisfactory options and solutions, use professional resources such as advertising agencies, marketers, or graphic designers to assist you. Don't gamble or guess. Whenever you come up with a vague answer, go back to the beginning. Don't experiment with your future. You should know you will succeed before you begin. Creating a new persona is not a risky gamble. Your plan should be carefully researched and analyzed and tested so that the results are very predictable.

What to Do When

Finally, set your priorities. List your solutions in order of importance, beginning with the liabilities that are related to the more important Persona Factors: Image, Reality, Customization, Credibility, Compromise, Growth, Research, and Independence. Then address the most severe liabilities. Always deal with the Persona Factors before the Persona Codes. Determine if time, seasonality, or competition makes execution urgent or casual.

For example, through your informal Persona Inventory you may have determined that you need moderate improvement to your image (Persona Factor 1, the Image Factor) and major improvement to your Credibility (Persona Factor 4, the Credibility Factor). You may have found that you have no testimonies from your clients indicating your superiority (Persona Code 37, Code of Testimony) and your price is considered very high (Persona Code 81, Code of Price). Your prospects do not know you by name (Persona Code 8, Code of Recall) and you do not own any claim in your target audience's mind (Persona Code 14, Code of Ownership). Which issue do you tackle first? Well, to begin with, you automatically start with the factors. In the above example, you might decide to address your liabilities in this order:

- ★ Image
- ★ Credibility
- ★ Price
- ★ Ownership
- ★ Testimony
- ★ Recall

The last step in your planning process is to develop a detailed, step-by-step priority list that details the solutions you have decided to employ to transform your liabilities. This list should be organized in order of execution, in as detailed a fashion as possible. In the above example, you might list these steps:

- ★ Develop a new logo with the help of an award-winning graphic artist to improve image.
- ★ Add the tag line "FCAC approved" to every communication to enhance credibility.
- ★ Raise price marginally, to test response to the claim of greater durability.
- ★ Create a positioning statement unique to the company within the industry.
- ★ Actively solicit testimonials from happy clients and use their statements in advertising.
- ★ Improve recall in the target audience by increasing the frequency of advertising through the advertising agency. Because of a limited budget, go from full-page four-color ads to half-page ads, but maintain color to capture potential clients' attention.

Executing Your Plan

You now have a basic plan of action—a rough, homemade Persona Plan. If you feel comfortable with this level of planning, execute your plan faithfully. Consider your Persona Credibility Index and Persona Compromise Quotient in the execution.[27] If you have a Persona Credibility Index (PCI) below 1, your plan should include some elements of excitement: exciting claims, headlines, offers, guarantees, and image. If your PCI is above 1, you must consider conservative Reverse-Imaging techniques: easily proven claims, credible advertising, straightforward messages. Your Persona Compromise Quotient (PCQ) will indicate how rigid you must be in your planning.

If your PCQ was below 10, we strongly advocate a formal Persona Inventory and Persona Plan.[28]

You should consider using experts to execute those steps of your plan that are outside your expertise. You might hire graphic artists to create a graphic image for your company. You would consider a strategic advertising agency to help you determine how best to reach your audience. You could engage a public relations expert to help you build credibility through strategic news releases. You might hire a mail house to distribute your new image brochure.

Informal, homemade Persona Plans may work as well as the formal techniques of the *Persona Planning Guide,* and they may be more suitable to entrepreneurs who dislike mathematics and in-depth research. If you are happy with your self-made plan, you will likely succeed. The advantage of creating your own system is that you can customize your answers. However, the danger is that your customization may result in a plan created through incorrect assumptions. Your own personal prejudices may influence the answers in your informal inventory and plan. Be certain about your assumptions and ask an impartial expert to review your plans before execution.

Persona by
the Book

▼

"Structure without life is dead.
But life without structure is un-seen."
John Cage
Silence

We strongly advocate the formal Persona Plan, as it offers a number of advantages:

★ The questions are standardized and force the entrepreneur to research the situation thoroughly.

★ The questions are based on mathematical models that index all ventures to one standard.

★ The standardized numbers are meaningful and interpreted for you.

★ Liabilities are rated numerically, providing a more scientific method of setting priorities.

★ The rigid format of the Persona Planning Guide takes into account all aspects of your venture's image.

★ You can measure your success by repeating the Persona Inventory at regular intervals to see how the ratings have improved.

★ The rigid format has been proven through considerable empirical and clinical testing involving more than 162 ventures of all types and sizes.

Many students of Persona have developed their own brilliant concepts in the process of taking a formal Persona Inventory of their venture. The process of discovery, research, and auditing your resources, your competitors' resources, and your market environment is the single most important thing you can do to ensure your success. The formal Persona Plan is anchored in the Persona Inventory.

The most precise method of developing an effective Persona Plan is to use the Persona Planning Guide. You are taken, step-by-step, through a professional marketing system. The consistency of the planning process is what makes the Persona Principle so powerful. There are three major indexed ratings to the Persona Process:

★ Persona Credibility Index (PCI) determines your credibility to your target audience and must be completed first.[29]

★ Persona Compromise Quotient (PCQ) indicates your willingness to compromise and must be completed second.[30]

★ Persona Inventory Composite (PIC) is a measure of your "venture-worthiness" and gives you a precise indication of the strength of your assets versus that of your liabilities. This number is a clear indication of how much planning you will have to undertake and clearly indicates which liabilities must be addressed first. By repeating the PIC every six months, you will have a precise indicator of your progress or lack of progress.

The Persona Planning Process also makes use of other yardsticks, including:

★ Persona Motivation Rating (PMR), which gauges your reasons for undertaking the Plan and your motivation for succeeding.

★ Persona A & L Ratio (PAL), which is a direct measurement of your Persona Liabilities against your Persona Assets.

★ Persona Composite Credit Rating (PCCR) is a composite rating similar to that of many credit rating agencies, which precisely measures your current credit situation.

★ Total Adjusted Aggression Shortfall (TAAS), which tells you very precisely how far you have to go to achieve your goal.

★ Persona Gross Reach Point (PGRP) represents as a cumulative (or gross) number how much reach you need in your audience to obtain your stated objectives.

If all of these indexes and ratings seem intimidating, you might want to conduct your own informal audit and plan using the recommendations we have discussed in Your Own Persona Planning Technique. However, any venture that conducts a full Persona Inventory and Plan will be better equipped to profit from their market than a venture that does not. You will know more about your competition when you are finished, and you will have a set of ratings that are meaningful guideposts for future action.[31] This doesn't mean, of course, that the formal Persona Plan is right for every venture. You should consider a formal Plan if:

★ Your venture is a start-up.

★ Your venture has enjoyed no growth for a prolonged period of time.

★ You are considering a venture and want to determine feasibility.

★ Your venture is declining in market share or revenues.[32]

★ Your venture has grown so large you feel you have lost control of or are "out of touch" with the customer.

★ Your competitors have initiated an aggressive image or marketing campaign that you feel may damage your bottom line.

The Formal Persona Inventory

The formal Persona Inventory is over 100 pages long and takes at least six weeks to complete.[33] Since accuracy is crucial, you should not undertake it lightly. Your success depends on a full understanding of your market.

The Persona Inventory is the most important element of the Persona Planning Process. Without complete and accurate knowledge of your current situation, you cannot decide how to improve. Similarly, without total knowledge of your competitors' situation, you cannot see your opportunities. If you are serious about your success, you should obey this marketing maxim:

Marketing is 90 percent research and 10 percent action.

Effective image flows from effective research. While you can have a great creative idea without research, it probably won't be effective. Only strategic creative or marketing initiatives add value to your venture.

The Formal Persona Plan

The Persona Inventory is your foundation. The Persona Plan is the building. If built on a strong foundation, your Plan will succeed. If your foundation is full of inaccuracies and guesses, you cannot expect success. Only completely accurate answers that are researched, rather than assumed, can lead to a foolproof Persona Plan.

You should think of your Persona Plan as a war plan. Like any great commander, you must execute your plan faithfully, without compromise and without mercy.

There are five major steps to the Persona Plan:

★ **Section A—Where You Are Now**: A complete summary of your assets, liabilities, and ratings from the Persona Inventory in an easy-to-follow one-line-per-item format.

★ **Section B—Where You Are Going**: A comprehensive system for setting objectives, rating options, and choosing actions.

★ **Section C—Persona Aggression Plan**: A step-by-step guide to determining "lift" based on the numeric system of the Persona Inventory and your specific goals. This aggressiveness rating sets the priorities in your Persona Plan. Your overall Total Adjusted Aggression Shortfall (TAAS) will tell you how aggressive your plan must be.

★ **Section D—Your Persona Weapons**: In this section, you will rate your potential weapons according to these standards: message, impact, reach, recall, frequency, and response. You will index these standards to the priority of your goals. This section will help you choose your weapons for the Persona War you are about to fight.

★ **Section E—Your Persona Plan**: This section is mostly mathematics. Using all of your inventoried ratings, you will calculate your Persona Gross Reach Points goal (PGRP) and set forth steps to success. You will address each weakness of your Persona Inventory and create a plan for treating all liabilities step-by-step, in order of priority.

Making Persona
Work for You

▼

*"The honors and rewards fall to those
who show their good qualities in action."*
Aristotle

Nichomachean Ethics

Once you have your Persona Plan—formal or informal—it's time for action. Any plan—from business to Persona—that is not enacted is only an academic exercise of no tangible value. The rewards will only come to those "who show their good qualities in action."

To execute a plan, there are basically three methods:
★ Use only your internal resources.
★ Use your internal resources where you can, then consultants when you need extra help.
★ Use experts for each of the important stages of persona development.

Although the Persona Principle is a self-help guide, we strongly advocate the use of professional consultants. Your Persona Plan identifies the steps, but some of the steps may require professional help to fulfill the high standards of Persona. Whether you need professional assistance will depend on your own skills. However, to be number one, you must look like number one. To look like number one, you sometimes have to hire number one.

Remember the maxim "Marketing is 90 percent research and 10 percent action." If you have completed a well-researched Persona Plan, you have the 90 percent solution. You need to invest in professional help only for the remaining 10 percent.

Hiring a Persona Doctor
You should consider an outside consultant or expert, a Persona Doctor, if any of the following are true:
★ I have the expertise to execute the plan step but am unable to do so because of other commitments.
★ I have some expertise but am not an expert.
★ I have no expertise.

A Persona Doctor is an important investment. You should take the same care in hiring an image consultant that you would in consulting a medical doctor. The health and success of your business is at stake. Just as you wouldn't consider self-diagnosis for a life-threatening ailment, you should not consider self-execution of a Persona Plan step.

Any liability which is related to a Persona Factor—Image, Credibility and so on—should be solved by an expert. Your image and credibility are fundamental to your success. You may know how to make the best ball bearings available, but you are probably not capable of producing the best logo for your ball-bearings company.

Hire Only The Best

As with a medical doctor, you must hire only the best you can afford. You do not want a doctor fresh from medical school performing open-heart surgery. Similarly, you do not want a fresh-from-arts-school graphic artist creating your all-important logo.

Budget what you can afford based on your priorities. Liabilities that stem from major Persona Factors should be allocated a larger budget than those that involve the less important Persona Codes.

Contrary to popular belief, the Yellow Pages are a terrible source of "Persona Doctors." Trade association lists are better, and recommendations from a highly satisfied associate are even better. The best approach to finding the best consultants is to ask for a capabilities presentation from those who are referred by someone you trust. Check them out with the Better Business Bureau and their own trade associations. Examine their work. The first test is whether their past work appeals to you. The most important test, however, is if it worked. When you are shown past work, ask for the specific results. Don't settle for a vague, unsupported answer such as "It really worked. The client is very happy." Find out how much growth the consultant's idea resulted in. How much revenue was produced? Are the clients still using the program?

Look especially for suppliers who:
★   Are written up in their own trade media as experts.
★   Have a portfolio of work that appeals to you.
★   Have a portfolio of work that shows expertise in your
     need area.[34]

- ★ Have several years of experience as an expert.
- ★ Can provide at least three references.
- ★ Have been recognized by their peers through awards or accolades.
- ★ Can offer real case histories with measurable results.

The last criterion is probably the most important. Results matter. There can be no excuse for failure. We define results as achieving or surpassing the objectives of the client. Winning awards is not the same as achieving results; it only indicates skill. Client revenue results are the only true measure of a successful strategy. You want a doctor who can cure you—not a doctor who is famous. Fame may be an indication of skill, and skill is important to the cure, but ultimately only the final results count.

Never hire a Persona Doctor on spec. A doctor who gets paid only if he provides a cure does not try harder. In this situation, a doctor can play a numbers game: try this, try that until something works. You need a skilled and knowledgeable practitioner who has a proven track record and offers a tailored strategy. You do not need pretty pictures and cool graphics.

Practitioners who work on spec usually represent the bottom tier of any profession. They work on spec because they have to; meanwhile, the best always charge high fees. They research a problem before proposing an idea and offer the best offer solutions, not neat ideas. Generally, the more you pay, the more you get. Consultants work as many hours as you'll pay them for. If you pay them less, they'll give you less, resulting in either a less effective strategy or a greater demand on your internal resources.

Any component of your plan that is exposed to your audience should be professionally executed by a carefully chosen Persona Doctor. These components include:

★ Graphic design: logos, wordmarks, advertising design, packaging design, point-of-purchase design, annual report design, stationery design, brochure and publicity kit design, and so on.

★ Interior design: any work environment that your audience will be exposed to.

★ Advertising: advertising copy, media planning, positioning statements, branding strategies.

★ Public relations.

★ Various suppliers: sign makers, videographers, photographers, and so on.

Giving Birth to Persona

The most important step in creating a persona is the act of giving birth. The Persona Plan provides the building blocks of the persona. The persona should have a life of its own—fully independent of the creator. Like a child, the persona must learn how to act, what is right and wrong, and how to grow. This is not a vague concept. Persona is an identity. Once you or your venture assumes that identity, the persona develops a virtual life. You give birth to the persona when you launch your persona imagery, which includes:

★ Your company or brand name.

★ Your company or brand logo.

★ Your company signage, stationery, and advertising.

★ Your brand packaging.

Nurturing Persona

The persona will grow in faster leaps than a child would. Because a persona's life is planned and the route is sure, success is inevitable. But to sustain and maximize success, persona must be nurtured, coaxed, encouraged—even bribed at times! Its growth will be rapid, provided the creator is consistent, aggressive, and serious.

The most important way to nurture a persona is to follow a carefully formulated and detailed plan. From the way your phone is answered to the price you put on your product or service, you must plan your future. Nothing is left to chance in the Persona Plan. Every action is designed for your specific goals. You will set a dress code for your staff. You will have a corporate standard for your stationery. You will have an advertising strategy that must be strictly adhered to. You will train your staff to respond to your audience in specific ways.

Over time, these rules that were once so onerous become your company's culture. Until you have a culture that no longer requires the discipline of rules, you must nurture your growing persona. Once your culture is entrenched, you have a mature persona with valuable equity.

Setting Persona Free

After a very rapid nurturing, it is time to set the young adult free. Your persona deserves to live. Every slip of the tongue, every time you say "my intention" instead of "my persona's intention" will weaken the value of the persona. You now have a culture. Your culture will be infectious. New employees will become quickly absorbed into it, and clients will be attracted by it. No one will remember or care how it all started. Your persona will become a living creature that can make its own choices—based on programmed responses.

Now is the time to set persona free.

Create Your Own Luck

Success is created by strategy, never by luck. You are not going to win a lottery. You are not going to be noticed by accident. You make your own luck. The power of Persona is that you can plan your success. You can know, before you begin, that you will succeed.

There are more than eight million self-employed business people and entrepreneurs in the United States alone. Either directly or indirectly, they are competing for your market. There are almost two million business services salespeople in America who are doing their best to convince your market to spend on a different service from yours. Simultaneously, more than five million retail salespeople and one and a half million commodities sales representatives are battling for a share of your market's money. And finally, almost 400,000 advertising professionals are trying to get your audience to notice someone else's product instead of yours.[35] The Persona Principle can help you succeed against these terrifying odds.

Persona will help you overcome the biggest obstacles to your success: invisibility and incredibility. Following the strategies and advice outlined in this book will make your venture visible and credible and can bring you heretofore elusive success.

Marketing is a war as deadly and as ruthless as any military struggle. You are at a disadvantage from the day you decide to pursue your entrepreneurial goals. The Persona Principle gives you the advantage of proven weaponry for this battle. Consistent, uncompromising, faithful application of your Persona Plan should bring you success in this fierce war. Know your enemy, know your persona, live your persona, and you can win your battles and, eventually, your war.

Appendix

Getting Help with Persona

Building Persona is a complex process. This book has introduced you to the basic concepts, history, and application of the Persona Principle. You can benefit greatly from an understanding of the concepts just by reading and rereading them. You have learned how to create your own informal Persona Inventory and Persona Plan. You can already calculate your Persona Credibility Index and Persona Compromise Quotient from the exercises in this book.

If you apply the Persona Factors and Persona Codes in this book, you can drastically change the way you market your venture. No marketing technique has more power than Image-Marketing, and no Image-Marketing process is more effective than the Persona Principle.

As we have mentioned, to gain the full benefit of a Persona Plan, you should consider undertaking the formal Persona Principle Planning Process. These techniques are proven and have a 100 percent success track record. There are four ways to pursue formal Persona Planning:

★ Attend one of the public Persona Seminars.
★ Arrange for a customized corporate workshop.
★ Complete the self-help method by using the *Persona Planning Guide.*
★ Hire a consultant to complete the formal *Persona Planning Guide.*

For information on these methods, or to subscribe to our quarterly newsletter, contact:

The Persona Principle Inc.
88 Advance Road
Toronto, Canada
M8Z 2T7
1-800-508-4333

The authors are interested in your feedback and your case studies. Please send us information on your particular case and how you used Persona in your business, your profession, or your personal life to achieve your goals. Your story may be used in our widely circulated newsletter, *The Persona News*.

Notes

1. Statistics are according to a 1995 survey conducted by *Advertising Age* magazine

2. All the important techniques are contained within this book. Detailed step-by-step formulas are contained in a separate workbook called the Persona Planning Guide. See Part Five of this book for information.

3. According to *Advertising Age* magazine, 1994.

4. For the complete Macintosh story, read Guy Kawasaki's entertaining *Selling the Dream*.

5. The Persona Credibility Index is the first exercise in the formal Persona Inventory Process. See Part 5—A Persona How-To. The PCI is not to be reproduced in any form without the permission of the authors and is protected by registered copyrights.

6. Your main positioning statement is crucial. If you do not have one for your venture, you should stop now and take as much time as necessary to determine what position your venture occupies in your audience's mind. For the purposes of this exercise, you should not develop a new positioning statement but try to determine *how your audience* perceives you *now*. A positioning statement is a one sentence description of how you are uniquely perceived by your target audience. Weak positioning refers to anything general, such as "We are a cola company." Stronger positioning statements are carefully defined, such as "We are the number one strawberry-flavored cola."

7. Define your main target carefully. Your main target is whoever buys—or you would like to buy—your offering. Describe this accurately, with as much detail as you can. For example: "Mostly females, aged 25–40, married with children or separated with children" is a well-defined main target.

8. Rating believability is a purely rational exercise. Don't judge your positioning statement for excitement, power, or any other factor. Rate only the credibility of the claim, based on the specific statements indicated, from the point of view of your main target audience. This can be done by informally phoning several clients (polling), focus groups with your audience, marketing surveys by a professional, or simply informal judgment (but only if you know the information for certain, based on extensive experience).

9. Your client share is defined very easily. Take your entire customer list and determine how many on the list are in your specific main target audience. This is not the same as market share. Client share is just a demographic breakdown of YOUR customers. If your billing system does not track clientele, you will have to undertake some basic marketing research. If you do not have any market share or clients (i.e., you have a start- up venture), your rating is zero in question 1, 2, and 3.

10. For example, if your rating in question one was 4 and your percentage of customers in this audience (of your total client base) is 50 percent, you multiply 4 by 50 and divide by 100 (or multiply 4 by 50 percent), equaling 2.

11. All ventures have a secondary and tertiary positioning statement. This is either informal and instinctive or formal and precise. If you do not know your secondary and tertiary statements, discover them now. The secondary and tertiary statements are different from your overall positioning statement in that they are directed at secondary and tertiary audiences. For example, in our cola example above, the secondary audience might be teenagers, so the secondary positioning might become "a radical taste for radical people."

12. This is a simple exercise. Add all your percentage scores in question 1, 2, and 3 and deduct from 100. This figure will represent the remaining market shares.

13. This does not refer to your main competitor's main target audience. Rate your competitor's position against your own target audiences. What we are looking for is the way your main audience sees your main competitor. You may know already, or you may need market research, but don't guess.

14. Generally your positioning statement reflects the substance of your offering. Here you are rating the need of your offering as you have positioned it to your audience. For example, "a wildly different cola experience" is not a need—or even a want —to a conservative audience. Rate only the need based on your positioning!

15. The first into the market usually owns first mind and therefore an advantage, unless the value is weakened by poor marketing. This rating gives credit to the first in, but deducts points for not keeping the number one spot. First in is only first in if you were clearly the first—and therefore inventor or originator—of a unique product.

16. This is a copyrighted document, protected by registered copyrights, and may not be reproduced in any form.

17. Short-term needs always compromise long term goals, without exception.

18. If you have not yet completed your PCI, you should do so first. The Persona Compromise Quotient and the Persona Inventory Composite Index require the PCI number.

19. In other words, if you would compromise for more than one of these reasons, take your lowest rating first, then subtract a numerical 1 for each additional pressure. For example, if you would compromise for "competitive pressure" and "client pressure," you would take the lowest rating of 3 and subtract one for your additional reason, leaving you with a final rating of 2.

20. You should have completed your Persona Credibility Index in the exercise under the Credibility Factor. Your Persona Credibility Factor is the most important calculation you can make in Persona Planning. If you have not completed this exercise, return to it now.

21. Be precise. If the numbers don't bear you out, answer False. If you are second place by a small margin, answer False. If you don't know and can't find out, answer False. If you are a start-up, answer False.

22. Nothing as nebulous as "we want to be number one." To answer true. you must have specific goals which are quantifiable and realistic.

23. Note the difference between question 2 and 4. One asks if your claim is true; the other asks if it is believable.

24. No qualified answers, please. Either you do or you don't. Unwritten verbal rules don't count, and part-time rule-breaking requires that you answer False.

25. If your company has been in existence fewer than four years, answer False.

26. If you do not research *everything*, from insignificant to important, answer False.

27. If you have not completed the exercises under the Credibility Factor and the No-Compromise Factor, we strongly recommend you do so now. Your PCI and PCQ ratings are fundamental to your success even if you do not undertake a formal Persona Inventory and Persona Plan.

28. You will need several weeks of dedicated time, and the Persona Planning Guide is expensive, but the investment is well worth it to any start-up or failing firm. Even if you are currently very successful, you will find the *Persona Planning Guide* a useful tool. For information on ordering, refer to the appendix.

29. The complete Persona Credibility Index is reproduced in the chapter on the Credibility Factor.

30. The complete Persona Compromise Quotient is reproduced in the chapter on the No-Compromise Factor.

31. We strongly advocate half-yearly Persona Inventory reviews. Comparing your indexed numbers from one review to the next can give you a precise measure of your progress. Start-ups or aggressive planners should consider quarterly reviews.

32. A decline in revenues is a strong motivation for conducting a number of audits—especially a Persona Inventory. A decline in profits, not resulting from a decline in revenues, is not likely to be image related, although an audit can't hurt. You may find your "culprit" in the process.

33. See the appendix for information on where to order your Persona Planning Guide.

34. This does not mean you should look for an ad agency that has promoted fried chicken just because you sell fried chicken. It does mean you should watch for innovative solutions to problems that are similar to your own. In fact, past experience in your specific industry can be a liability. Professionals who specialize too tightly tend to offer "off-the-shelf" solutions to industry problems instead of customized strategies based on research. This means that you could end up resembling your competitors' too closely, which violates the intent of the Code of First Mind.

35. These numbers are all rounded statistics from the U.S. Bureau of Labor 1992 report.